ADDIT O
·*ENDURI* G

"Joseph Minich's *Enduring Divine Absence* is a marvelous essay that deals with the underappreciated temptation or *psychological* pull of atheism, the *feeling* that atheism is still somehow plausible even for believers who are aware of atheism's intellectual problems. Minich thoughtfully analyzes this temptation, beginning with accurately and sympathetically explaining what it actually feels like (and I would know). He then gives insightful suggestions on some of its main causes, and ends by helpfully offering practical advice for those who feel it (who are more numerous than most of us realize). Again, Minich clearly understands those who are tempted in this way, gently assuring them that it is an entirely understandable feeling, but without going so far as to make doubt a positive, Promethean virtue that's necessary for "the journey of faith." I recommend this book to those who have nagging doubts about God's existence or have been surprised by the sting of an objection to Christianity. I greatly enefited from it."

—*Mitch Stokes, Senior Fellow of Philosophy, New Saint Andrews College.*

DAVENANT ENGAGEMENTS seek to creatively and critically apply the received wisdom of our historic Protestant tradition to modern intellectual and cultural challenges that we face in the twenty-first century.

ENDURING DIVINE ABSENCE

The Challenge of Modern Atheism

BY JOSEPH MINICH

Cover design by Rachel Rosales, *Orange Peal Design.*

For Samuel and Sam

CONTENTS

PREFACE

THIS LITTLE book has three origins. First, the content herein was initially delivered as a series of lectures in November of 2016 at Rochester Reformed Presbyterian Church in New York via the invitation of my dear friend, Rev. Patrick Stefan. My wife and I spent a wonderful weekend with his family (and his church's guests) as we pored over this material—followed by fine wine and intimate fellowship. This origin accounts for the conversational tone which survives the modification of the manuscript to be more fitted to the written rather than to the spoken word. In any case, I am profoundly grateful to Patrick for pulling this material out of me, as well as for his continued friendship and support.

Second, and more personally, this material was birthed in my (continued!) attempt to reflect upon, exegete, and cope with my own lifelong struggle with Christian belief—whether birthed in critical reflection or crisis. What is offered here is not in the spirit of recommending or justifying some parody of my individual psychology. Rather, I offer this in the hope that my own intellectual and spiritual path toward a deeper settledness of soul might aid some fellow pilgrim on the journey to Zion. I hope to expand upon many of these points in my forthcoming (Lord willing) doctoral dissertation in the Humanities at The University of Texas at Dallas.

Third (and finally), the most proximate origin of this volume is the kind solicitation of another dear friend, Dr. Brad Littlejohn, who had done me a great honor by making the publication of this volume possible—and a greater honor still in being excited about it. I am so thankful for Brad's work, as well as the work of The Davenant Institute more generally—both the urgent and useful material that it produces on behalf of Christ's kingdom, but (more personally) for giving utterance to a person whose musings might otherwise have never seen the light of day.

As these words are published, I am particularly thankful to the Reformed Irenics group for constant intellectual and spiritual stimulation. Without them, this book would either be non-existent or much inferior. I am also grateful for the years-long friendship of two atheist friends, David Kotlc and Merriman Zajac, who have challenged me and shaped my approach to this topic. Finally, without the formatting and editorial help of Dan Kemp, Onsi Kamel, Jonathan Roberts, and Josiah Roberts, this essay would be significantly less readable. I am grateful for their labors.

I dedicate this work to two persons. The first, Dr. Samuel Tullock, mentored and encouraged a young freshman to navigate through his doubts without fear—but rather with simple faith in reality and in the God who grounds it. The second is my son Sam—who has expressed primal philosophical and spiritual doubts since he was six. He is now eleven. I hope this volume will bless both of them. If these musings, by God's grace, aid any soul in finding a greater orientation in the gravity of our great God, I will have more than all the reward I could wish for.

I:

INTRODU CTORY REFLECTIONS

THIS MODEST essa attempts to address the problem of the *temptation* of athei m. This is to be distinguished from several other ways of pproaching the question of atheism as a theist generally o as a Christian specifically. My intent here is not, as such, to argue for the existence of God or to refute atheism. More importantly, my main inquiry is not just a question about or an analysis of athe*ists*. I am most immediately intereste in why those who are *not* atheists can still nevertheless understand why it is that atheism might be plausible to someone. Let us clarify this. There are plenty of person who are persuaded for all sorts of rational reasons that God exists or that atheism is not just wrong, but deeply an philosophically incoherent. I count myself among their number. And yet these same persons might confess to you hat the atheist vision of an apathetic universe, of a cosmo which reduces to impersonal forces, (etc.) nevertheless retains some psychological pull and continues to resurfac as an intellectual item which "must be dealt with" thro ghout their lives. If you do not recognize yourself in this sort of experience, then this essay will possibly be less interesting for you—something

1

like a museum exhibit of interesting (or at least pitiable) people. For the rest of us poor souls, I'd like to move even more narrowly within the larger question of atheistic plausibility, and do so initially by telling a story—a tempting vice which I promise not to overly indulge.

I could tell a lot of stories which highlight how this issue has come home for me personally, but I think one in particular exposes my own (and I suspect our) vulnerability. I worked in Rockville, Maryland at the time, and I was driving home listening to NPR (because, of course, that's supposed to make you a smart person). In any case, the radio show I found myself listening to highlighted a story about an "agnostic" or "atheist" Jr. High camp—an apparent twenty-first century parody of our more beloved Bible camps. As this story unfolded, an NPR journalist interviewed one of the camp's attendees, a bright-sounding young lady of 12 or 13 years. After a little bit of back and forth with the interviewer, this young woman was afforded the opportunity to present one of her skeptical missiles and it went something like this (I'm paraphrasing, mind you):

> You know, God could totally get rid of all atheism if He'd just show up. I mean, think of it. How hard would it be for the Almighty to peel back the clouds every day at 3:00 PM for 'God time' and say, 'Hey, guys. Here I am. See ya.' If he did that? No atheism. So why doesn't he if we're supposed to believe in Him?

It is perhaps unadvisable, wanting to seem intelligent to my readers, to admit that the juvenile musings of a 12-

year-old girl at agnostic camp actually made me feel a bit dumb—like Moses turning his staff into a serpent and then being at least slightly shown up by Pharaoh's wizards. But advisability be damned. I was hit—a seminary student who did nothing but think about religion and atheism schooled by a 12-year old at atheist camp on the radio.

Of course, the story didn't end there. My world didn't come "colliding down." I had all the typical intellectual and not-so-intellectual reactions (ranging from reasons why I knew God existed to more self-assuring reactions that 'of course' such reasoning was juvenile). But the point of this story is not to dwell upon my own psychology. It is rather to highlight where I suspect a lot of us are at. I suspect that this little dart hits a lot of us in the gut, and what I want to explore in this little piece is *why* that is. Specifically, and we could explore the topic in many ways, but specifically, why does divine absence bother us precisely in relationship to *this* question (of God's existence)? Why does the fact that God does not show up in a certain concrete manner have any relevance for the question of His existence? That we don't see Him when we pray, that He often seems distant, that sometimes our prayers bounce off the ceiling, and especially for suffering people, that sometimes we can beg for Him to just "show Himself" to us, and He doesn't—all of this causes us to *feel* or at least be tempted to feel that maybe His non-existence is the most "natural" inference. Sometimes the universe, our experiences—let's get concrete—our marriages, our relationships, (etc.) feel as though they are lived out in the face of a deafening divine silence, and *therefore* a divine vacuum—all reduced to an indifferent cosmos (deaf to our prayers, joys, and pains). I say "sometimes." This could all, of course, be qualified. But my goal here is to acknowledge and (like the Psalmist) give utterance to those moments when it is *barely* qualified, those moments where belief even in the basic notion that God *is* at all feels difficult— and feels difficult for precisely these reasons.

I will make one final preliminary comment, and then give a broad outline of the material I plan to cover. That final preliminary comment is this: We need to recognize the distinctively historical character of the problem as I have stated it. Persons have always struggled with divine absence in various forms, and there is a significant degree of continuity between the Psalmist's "Where are you, God?" and our own struggles with atheism. But there is also a significant difference. To wit, neither the Psalmist, the Ancient Near Eastern pagan, medieval Catholic, nor the ancient starving Chinese peasant thought that their unanswered cries to the silent sky had any relevance to the question of whether God exists or not. That God existed was an obvious truth written into the fabric of basic phenomenological and social experience. Charles Taylor helps us to understand the significance of the modern condition in his magisterial *A Secular Age*.[1] Taylor argues that the Middle Ages, for instance, represent a moment in which disbelief in God was simply not plausible. It is not that one could not ask the question of whether God existed or not *technically*, as Thomas Aquinas does in his *Summa Theologica*. But it is that no-one's belief in God was suspended atop understanding Thomas' arguments. Even if his arguments were all refuted, it was still "obvious" (in some very relevant sense) that God existed. What has

---

[1] Charles Taylor, *A Secular Age* (Cambridge: Belknap Press, 2007).

changed now is not, 'aylor argues, that we can no longer believe in God. We can. We can find reasons for God rationally compelling. But *what it is like* to believe, or the *experience* of believing, is the experience of taking one option among many in respect of the God question. Not believing in God is plausible (i.e. has a pull), or is a "living option" in the taxonomy of William James—even if we reject that option.[2] This is profoundly important for our analysis. To live in a world in which belief is felt to be one living option among many is simply to live in a world in which an alternative belief is very possibly (at least psychologically) *plausible* to us, or somehow faintly understandable to us in a way that it simply was not to many of our ancestors.

For our purposes, I will leave aside the question of whether or not there are precedents for the distinctive character of modern atheism in ancient Western philosophy or in other traditions. I would argue that most of the items so-claimed as precedent were front-loaded with metaphysical speculation that most modern atheists in the West would consider, on the face of it, quasi-religious, but this does not necessarily matter for my analysis. We can at least agree that this has not been a living option in recent memory in the West—and that it now is.[3]

[2] I borrow this phrase from James' essay, "The Will to Believe," originally published in 1896 and preserved in many anthologies of his writing. For James, a "living option" is an option that seems open and vibrant to persons. That is, it is available to them in a way that is not just theoretical, into which category we might put our technical ability to believe in the existence of Thor.

[3] On the rise of unbelief in the modern West, see Michael Buckley, *At the Origins of Modern Atheism* (New Haven: Yale University Press, 1987), and James Turner, *Without God, Without Creed: The Origins of Unbelief in America* (Baltimore: Johns Hopkins University Press, 1986).

For all intents and purposes, our problematic is a modern one. To wit, how is it possible that we can both (a) think we have compelling reasons to believe in God, and (b) even find atheism incoherent or obviously false in many ways, and yet (c) still *feel* it to be a living option? Said a little differently, why does it sometimes feel like it takes great *effort* to believe things about reality that are supposed to be obvious—as though we're holding onto it by an act of will rather than by a passive sense of its obviousness (the way it does not take a great act of will, for instance, to believe that you are reading this essay right now)? And why is the simple fact of divine absence even relevant to such a question—rather than a triviality which is related to other questions (theodicy, personal comfort)? How does it have any relevance for questions concerning God's being at all?

I aim to get at these questions in three steps. First (in chapter 1), I want to think more carefully about the simple *fact* of this problem, as well as to give a sampling of its inflection from a variety of sources. I would also like to entertain several interpretations of the phenomenon and give reasons why I think they are inadequate. I will then (in chapter 2) explore what is, in my judgment, a more proper historical explanation for and philosophical response to this conundrum. As stated above, my intention is not necessarily apologetical in this essay, but I will find it useful to clarify why someone might find claims for God's existence to be rationally persuasive and yet juxtapose the rational acceptance of philosophical arguments with the reality that God's existence has often seemed obvious without understanding them. What is more, it is often *now* not felt to be obvious even *with* them. The effect of this analysis, I would argue, will be deflationary for the atheist option. By this, I mean that this argument will, I hope, help us to understand both why atheism might feel plausible to us, and why its plausibility might have little to do with its being warranted or true. Finally (in chapter 3), I will ask what a particularly Christian analysis of our situation might be. What should we do now? Should we seek to move back to a situation where this is not a problem at all? Or are there resources within the Christian tradition for offering an alternative response? Indeed, from a Christian perspective, is the current pistic situation more an opportunity than a problem? I will argue that indeed, it is. But all this for later. For now, let's attempt to get inside the problem itself a little more holistically.

II:

MODERNITY AND DIVINE ABSENCE

IN THIS chapter, I would like to give a smattering of evidence that divine absence, the simple fact that God's being and activity are not as immediately obvious as the fact that you are reading this right now, is perceived by many moderns to be a problem. And because of this, belief is often portrayed as a matter of great intellectual and spiritual effort, whereas unbelief is tacitly felt to be the default intellectual position once we, to bastardize a Psalm, "cease striving and know that there is no God."

THE BASIC PHENOMENON

A few general observations are in order. In the last century, there have been many books in the philosophical community on themes related to the meaning of "presence" (often the presence of the transcendental) which have an almost sermonic flavor. George Steiner's *Real Presences* is perhaps a key text—reflecting a much

wider philosophical d scourse.[1] There are similar themes in
the works of Roge Scruton and Charles Taylor—a
tendency toward a view of religion which explicitly
addresses the absenc of God and seeks to climb the
(often) phenomenolo ical mountain to behold or a-behold
(with apophatic wor ler) the "line between the lines,"
Heidegger's "betweer ness," Levinas' "face," or Rudolph
Otto's "holy"—that we know not what" that is perhaps
best identified, as one of my friends is fond of putting it, as
"Whoa!"[2] Not being ble to take "presence" for granted,
there has been a su feit of popular religious works on
doubt as a virtue ra her than a vice[3] alongside a large
amount of popular orks on epistemology and proving
the existence of God—indeed, enough interest in
apologetics to get th impression that the status of one's
belief might actually epend upon it. Whether stated with
confident feeling or r ot, God does not appear to be all so
obvious. Not that thi is innate in apologetics, but the *ethos*
of much recent apol getics is demonstrably anxious and
reactive—an attempt at a sort of intellectual therapy for

---

[1] George Steiner, *Real P sences* (Chicago: The University of Chicago Press, 1986).

[2] On this, see David Bent y Hart, *The Beauty of the Infinite: The Aesthetics of Christian Truth* (Grand pids: Eerdmans, 2003) and *The Experience of God: Being, Consciousness, Bl* (New Haven: Yale University Press, 2013).

[3] In the now somewha dated works of the "emerging church" movement (Brian McLare etc.), and among their modern progressivist analogues (Peter Enns, F chel Held Evans, etc.) one often gets the impression that certainty is inherently suspicious and that doubt is innately valid fuel for the j urney of faith (a beloved metaphor). What is possibly obscured here a illicit doubts (James 1:6). Not wanting to focus upon the distinctio between illicit and non-illicit doubts, I here rather draw attention to th simple *fact* of this distinction.

the vulnerable.[4] One does not, after all, write a bunch of books on proving the existence of what is taken for granted, such as chairs, relationships, or the movie *Ghostbusters*. And where the apologetics strategy for coping with God's absence is *abandoned*, there are many recent attempts to carve a space for a more subtle religion by an argument for religious experience or consciousness, for a kind of delighted ambiguity. Surely we can hold onto just this one thing—this one slice of our own inaccessible subjectivity.[5]

What I'd want us to note here is precisely this sense of "preserving just this one thing." One gets the impression that, for many persons, human thought has chipped away at this and that religious fantasy, and that many religious persons have retreated to a smaller and smaller corner. In the final analysis, "Can we not just preserve our own experience, our own sense that we participate in absolute beauty—or must we reduce even

---

[4] Not a week goes by without a new monograph on "evidence" for God from intelligent design or some new journalistic style "discovery" of the evidence for the veracity of Scripture. I do not discount the value of these works as such. Rather, I only highlight their relationship to modern faith. I have known several persons who claimed that one of these popular works transformed their life. The question then becomes what happens if scholars identify "problems" in them. The works of Buckley and Turner (mentioned in footnote 3 of the previous chapter) argue, interestingly, that the rise of unbelief is traceable to the rise of modern apologetics. As soon as God became an item requiring defense, there is always the implicit possibility that the defense could fail.

[5] The "one thing" often held onto often takes its cues from any remainder of public respect (or, minimally, non-hatred) one can garner from presumed experts on reality—or (what amounts to the same thing) converting the content of traditional religious language into something altogether different. These dynamics are captured brilliantly in J. Gresham Machen's classic 1923 work, *Christianity and Liberalism,* as well as C.S. Lewis' novel, *That Hideous Strength.*

this to the goings on of naturally selected neurons which ultimately themselves reduce to the accidents of collapsed quantum waves?" I is precisely because this is the perceived situation th t much apologetics writing could be seen as a sort of *strate ic* attempt to "take back an area" that was taken away, wh ther it be fighting evolution with intelligent design and six-day creationism, relativism with absolutes, reason vith revelation, naturalism with philosophy, neutralit with presuppositionalism, and so forth. And yet, argual ly, what none of these attempts gets at (at least essentially is the very sense of fragility itself. Assumed and at stake in these debates, arguably, is the *felt* fragility of our deep st identities and truths—which are then surrounded by he hedges of argument, apologetic, practice, etc.

This felt fragilit is manifest, I'd argue, in many de-conversion narratives which fascinatingly (at least in our culture) often work in the following way: Someone converts from the ery complex *set* of claims that is Christianity all the wa to atheism (or vice versa) in one fell swoop. It is actually i ot as common, from what I can tell, for people to land in he middle (though it used to be that someone might conv rt to deism or to some even lesser heresy). But there is a sense in the modern discussions that "at stake" are whole stems, and this means that not only is the center vulnera le, but the whole structure can feel like a delicate house of cards wherein the foundational card is not so much protected by all the cards around it as rendered exponentia y more vulnerable for having so many areas of expos re. God's existence isn't felt only to depend upon Aquina , but upon whether the Bible can be falsified, whether the resurrection happened, or whether Moses wrote Genesis.

To lose belief, in this context, often feels very much like "letting go" or "coming to terms with" what can really be known and counted on. This dynamic is hauntingly portrayed in the recent film, *Higher Ground* (Farminga, 2011), which is based upon Carolyn S. Briggs' auto-biographical account of her own loss of faith, *The Dark World: A Memoir of Salvation Found and Lost.*[6] The film does not portray an intellectually or spiritually rebellious woman who "quits the church" because it was mean. It actually portrays a woman desperate to experience God, desperate to know that all things are in His control, desperate just to know that He is there. And what is she met with? Silence. Silence when she suffers spiritual abuse. Silence when her friend decays from cancer. Silence when her marriage begins to fall apart. Her eventual loss of faith is not felt to be a "decision," but a chased wind that ultimately gets away from her. In short, it simply stops seeming real or even plausible. Another version of this can be found in the surprisingly deep film, *The Grey* (Carnahan, 2011). In this film, a fairly rustic group of oil men are in a plane crash in the middle of the Alaskan wilderness. Like many movies of this sort, the better portion of the film involves their attempt to escape various dangers. What makes this story unique, however, are the explicit theological conversations that go on between the characters. Many of them are religious, but the main protagonist (wonderfully portrayed by Liam Neeson), who had previously watched his wife slowly die of cancer, while sympathetic to the impulse to

---

[6] Carolyn S. Briggs, *The Dark World: A Memoir of Salvation Found and Lost* (New York: Bloomsbury, 2002).

believe, nevertheless cannot *bring himself to* (and that's just how I'd want to say it)—cannot *get into a place where*—he can believe, even for cathartic reasons. For him, it would apparently be dishonest. The disaster scenario and its beautiful <u>surrounding scenery is a perfect way to communicate a universe that is at once full of wonder</u>, but <u>also full of hostility</u>—the balance of which is the cosmos's utter indifference to these small homo sapiens fumbling around in the snow. At the film's climax, Neeson looks up into the sky and screams in desperation, "Do something. Do something! You phony prick fraudulent motherf*****! Come on! Prove it. F*** faith. Earn it! Show me something real. I need it now. Not later. Now! Show me and I'll believe in you until the day I die. I swear. I'm calling on you. I'm calling on you!" The sky is silent. A tough Irishman, Neeson stands up and says, "F*** it. I'll do it myself." And yet, doing it oneself does not always work in the indifferent cosmos. Perhaps no film has captured an indifferent cosmos better than that incredibly beautiful but incredibly disturbing art piece by Lars Von Trier, *Melancholia* (2011). Aptly titled (it is quite depressing), the film opens at a wedding, but a wedding that is oppressively brooding. It is not for a while that the film-viewing audience realizes that this scene—which is supposed to be joyful—is juxtaposed to the wedding participant's awareness that a comet is coming toward the earth and is very likely to kill all living persons. The rest of the film, post-wedding, portrays the bride and her sister in a cottage preparing to see if the comet will strike the earth or slingshot around it. The film is full of waiting. Once it becomes clear that the comet will strike, the sisters build a little teepee in a field, sit in it with their children, and *wait*.

The film is interspersed with incredible scenes of natural beauty and cosmic wonder—but also of absolute indifference. All the joys and strife of human sentience will pass like a moment, like a breath, into the void of the cosmic sea.

This is at once disturbing, and yet it is not felt (though perhaps thought) by most of us to be insane. It is haunting. And the fact that it has this pull can cause us to question everything. How can I be so certain that this cosmic indifference is not the case? Indeed, just staring at the vastness of the cosmos juxtaposed to the smallness of my human mind, I wonder at how I can make confident pronouncements at all. *We... I...* am scandalously particular and limited and finite.

And yet, there is a sort of religious sentiment here. Nietzsche's defiant affirmation of life, this ability to stare such nihilism in the face and say "okay" and still receive it as beautiful—this itself is a kind of religious posture.[7] Indeed, one might view it as a covert atheist version of "pure actuality." Basically, the atheists are cheating. But let us forego this line of inquiry for the moment. When the atheist option became a bit more popular among intellectuals in the 19th century, it is fascinating to note how much of it had an aesthetic and existential appeal. Atheism could stare "nature red in tooth and claw" and yet simply wonder at its vastness, simply receive it in its most basic and unfiltered terms, with (again) a simple gratitude that human life *was* at all. Who cares where it comes from? Who cares if it's all just atoms banging together? It *is*! And

---

[7] Cf. Taylor's discussion of "subtler languages" throughout *A Secular Age*. See also Peter Watson's *The Age of Atheists: How We Have Sought to Live Since the Death of God* (New York: Simon & Schuster, 2014).

what can one do bu smile at this happy accident? The virtues required to ap reciate this are honesty and bravery. Therefore, it is only intellectually and existentially brave persons who can do his.[8] Here we see the appeal of this viewpoint as not just intellectual honesty for its own sake, but perhaps an even slightly self-indulgent self-evaluation that "I am able to tak it." This makes the view even more attractive. Not only d we cease striving, but we feel a kind of pure and basic level of cosmic wonder, *and* we get to feel the dignity of being honest and brave with reality as it coldly presents itself to us. It is indifferent. But we are those beautiful creatures who speak back to it and say, "I love you." Who cares if that doesn't "mean anything" ultimately? Who care if this is not founded on "absolute truth?" This posture is joy for its own sake. It is freedom and loss in wonder.

Again, I want to come back to this phenomenon later, but what I want to do for the moment is to allow us to admit to oursel es, if we dare, some degree of attractiveness about his option, an attractiveness which might be a bit self-indulgent and navel gazing (sure), but which cannot quite be reduced to these things. This is important for what will become my critique, because I don't think we can fully understand what is going on in modern atheism, at its best, unless we understand its aesthetic appeal as more than just the shallow stereotype of "being able to do whatever I want." It is far more than this. Its fundamental ethic, at its best, is one of honesty

---

[8] Here one thinks especially of Nietzsche's iconic "madman" announcing the death of God in the marketplace only to realize he has come too early for his pusillanimous fellows. The modern ethic of bravery was also captured in the title of Paul Tillich's famous 1952 work of Christian existentialism, *The Courage to Be.*

and a commitment to affirm life in the most basic fashion. We need not torture ourselves with all the odd particulars of dogma, but we can simply affirm the simplest things— that we are here after all, and that we must make do on this terrestrial ship in a vast cosmic sea. Indeed, in its modern form, atheism tends to terminate in an ethic similar to that which we find in John Lennon's justly famous 1971 song, *Imagine*. And for all the ways we could critique this song, who is not moved by its simple melody which presents to us its pleasant vision of our potential as humans on this earth? I daresay it is next to impossible for it not to strike a chord in us. The brotherhood of man? A world in which people care more about the good of their neighbor than the privilege of their nation? But included for Lennon in this is, "Imagine there's no heaven," which is *not* so striking as, "it's easy if you try." The latter renders it a modern song, indeed.

But, once again, this a-religion is itself irreducibly religious in sentiment. That sense that I can stare at the whole and say "whoa" is not simply explained *by* God, but it is, irreducibly, a religious posture. That before which we say "whoa" is that which we perceive to be bigger than us; it is that in which we are caught up, in which we are grounded, and which represents forces transcending our ordinary experiences and which—indeed (not to put too fine a point on it)—*gives* them to us.

One presumably liberating feature of this posture is its simplicity and clarity. In contrast to this, faith often feels like something we hold onto for dear life, but which ultimately eludes us. I recall a local convert from Roman Catholicism to Agnosticism in the Maryland area who wrote about his story of becoming an agnostic. And I recall that he used the image of his faith "losing steam." It was not that he didn' want to believe. He came to a point where he simply did not and could not. Despite his best efforts, he wrote as though he was effectively dragged into unbelief. This is not an uncommon phenomenon. I have met many atheists who tell a similar story. Perhaps no-one better described this than one of the 20th centuries great novelists, John Updike. Toward the beginning of his *In the Beauty of the Lilies*, he Presbyterian minister Clarence Wilmot is described a feeling "the last particles of his faith leave him. The sensation was distinct—a visceral surrender, a set of dark sparkling bubbles escaping upward."[9] Updike says later, "Clarence's mind was like a many-legged, wingless insect that had long and tediously been struggling to climb up the walls of a slick-walled porcelain basin; and now a sudden impatient wash of water swept it down into the drain. There is no God."[10] Clarence is stunned in this moment. Updike continues,

> Life's sounds all rang with a curious lightness and flatness, as if a resonating base beneath them had been removed. They told Clarence Wilmot what he had long suspected, that the universe was utterly indifferent to his states of mind as empty of divine content as a corroded kettle. All its metaphysical content had leaked away, but for cruelty and death, which without the hypothesis of a God became unmetaphysical; they became simply facts, which oblivion would in time

---

[9] John Updike, *In the Beauty of the Lilies* (New York: Fawcett Columbine, 1996), 5.

[10] John Updike, *In the Beauty of the Lilies*, 5-6.

obliviously erase. Oblivion became a singular comforter. The clifflike riddle of predestination—how can Man have free will without impinging upon God's perfect freedom? how can God condemn Man when all acts from alpha to omega are His very own?—simply evaporated; *an immense strain of justification was at a blow lifted. The former believer's habitual mental contortions decisively relaxed.* And yet the depths of vacancy revealed were appalling. In the purifying sweep of atheism human beings lost all special value. The numb misery of the horse was matched by that of the farmer; the once-green ferny lives crushed into coal's fossiliferous strata were no more anonymous and obliterated than Clarence's own life would soon be, in a wink of earth's tremendous time. Without Biblical blessing the physical universe became sheerly horrible and disgusting. All fleshly acts became vile, rather than merely some. The reality of men slaying lambs and cattle, fish and fowl to sustain their own bodies took on an aspect of grisly comedy—the blood-soaked selfishness of a cosmic mayhem. The thought of eating sickened Clarence; his body felt swollen in its entirety, like an ankle after a sprain, and he scarcely dared take a step, lest he topple from an ungainly height.[11]

Note what we see here. Clarence is not portrayed as *leaving* the faith. He did not *refuse* to believe. Faith and belief left *him* the way strength leaves the body. His will is

---

[11] John Updike, *In the Beauty of the Lilies*, 7, emphasis added. In interesting parallel to Updike's fascination with the body is his rather "clinical" poem, "Seven Stanzas on Easter."

portrayed as no more involved in losing this belief than it is in your will in affirming that you are conscious right now. You could hardly disbelieve this even if you *wanted* to! And Clarence could not believe even if he wanted to. Indeed, he laments his loss of faith at several points in the book, desperately wishing it was all true. And yet, the world seemed to him utterly different than the claims of faith. And so *faith* (rather than unbelief) was rendered an act of will and stubbornness—its absence the honest surrender to reality as it actually seemed.

And is this not how it can feel—that to believe is to *add* something to the undeniable features of reality, the common banality that we all recognize? To suffuse the cosmos with agency and intention and personality is felt to be something I must "try" to see rather than what is "obvious" to me otherwise.

COMMON INTERPRETATIONS

Before I move on to giving my own account of what I think the "main thing" is in this situation, I want to briefly entertain a few attempted explanations of this phenomenon, explain why I think they are ultimately defective (at least for the specific question before us), and then briefly state my own theses which I hope to unpack in the rest of this essay.

The first option, and perhaps the most obvious explanatory device for the above is that, well, these claims are plausible because the atheist option is the right one. I will spend more time on this claim in the next chapter, primarily arguing for why God is necessary and necessarily personal (but also hoping to explain that the atheist option still can feel natural and plausible to us). Nevertheless, I think we can offer a few preliminary responses along the following lines: Sometimes things seem plausible or obvious which are actually not so plausible or obvious. The reader's instinctive reaction might be, "Oh boy. This is the obvious truth and now this whole book is going to give excuses for avoiding reality." Misguided as this reaction is, I can't force anyone not to have it. But I can highlight some *prima facie* reasons for being careful here. For instance, there are those who have thought about this, who are demonstrably intellectually honest and brave, and yet who are firmly persuaded that God exists and that He is the rewarder of those who seek Him. Frankly, a denial that such persons exist is either ignorant, dishonest, or can be dismissed as merely polemical (and insecurely so). Indeed, I would argue that the most intellectually honest atheists can actually struggle *with belief* just we struggle with unbelief.[12] That is, they can lie awake at night and wonder if there is personality after all behind the scenes. What is more, they can understand why someone might take this option. Again, I speak of the most informed and the best atheists, not necessarily their juvenile counterparts. Atheists also live in a world in which God is a living option, and in which they can imagine "what it is like" to think of reality differently. Another consideration, as I began to say earlier, is that some things can seem plausible or obvious which, on reflection, are not so plausible or obvious. Atheists necessarily agree with this as it pertains to their medieval ancestors, for almost all of whom atheism was impossible. Commonly agreed upon historical

---

[12] On this, see Timothy Larsen's superb *Crisis of Doubt: Honest Faith in Nineteenth-Century England* (New York: Oxford University Press, 2009).

examples include the notion that the sun revolves around the earth, Aristotelians who argued that no species could go extinct (because no form could be without an existing instance), or pundits and people who argued that Donald Trump could not possibly become the Republican Nominee for the President of the United States. Current examples include the common (but clearly inadequate) reduction of gender to be entirely a social construct, the belief that religion masks "deeper motivations" whenever someone commits an act of evil in the name of religion, or the implausible fact that we *now* live in a world in which Donald Trump is the President of the United States!

A second way to grapple with the phenomenon we are describing is one which reduces all of these atheist temptations and conversions to a problem of the mind or of the will. Basically, people are tempted by or convert to atheism because they have bad ideas, or they are tempted by and convert to atheism because they have a distorted will. With respect to the former, the fix is normally to correct their ideas by persuading the temptee of truths and perspectives which will presumably take away the plausibility of atheism. With respect to the latter, the argument is often that such persons have a sinful will which opposes God and therefore have a great interest in God not existing. They are unable to be honest with reality because they want a lie to be true. I do not want to deny that there is truth in each of these observations or that there are many examples which could fit in each. But the same could be said the other way around. Are there believers who believe simply because God is a crutch, because they are afraid of the alternative, or for reasons other than true confidence, conviction, and clarity? Of course. But this is not true of all (or probably even average) believers. Similarly, I do not think the above adequately accounts for the atheist temptation on the whole. As it pertains to the mind, there are many persons (again) who are quite persuaded of the case for theism or Christianity for precisely the reasons that the objector is— but who still have difficulty shaking the possibility that atheism is true. This is *common*, and we need to account for and *minister* to it. With respect to the will, while it is true that human beings are in an ethical tension with God, this does not necessarily manifest itself in denying His existence or even in denying Christian theology. The demons believe and shudder, says James (2:19). Presumably, there are Westminster-confessing reprobates. While our tension with God might (and does!) cause us to distort reality, this does not account for the whole phenomenon, nor the fact that this is experienced by believers (who are pursuing God and in a right relationship to Him) as a very real temptation despite constant thought and prayer. This is a simple reality and it needs to be explained better than this.

It is important to reflect a bit more about this particular reaction because it is fairly common. Behind it is often a theology which implies that one cannot believe Christian truth apart from conversion. Sometimes this is felt to imply that substantive struggle with Christian truth must therefore reflect either the lack of conversion or its post-conversion approximation in remaining unbelief. This, is a deeply problematic claim because it inevitably reduces the persuasiveness and objective truth of Christian claims to a state of subjectivity. Even if Christ was raised from the dead in real history, our *persuasion* that He was raised from the dead is entirely dependent upon the right *subjective* starting point, a sort of special set of reality glasses which are not, then, *public* accessible. This therefore pushes Christian claims (qua common reality) out of their public vulnerability (or strength!) and into the subject. And this is a "retreat to commitment," to borrow a line from William Bartley.[13] In my judgment, this strategy is absolutely toxic to Christian confidence. I have similar concerns about apologetic attempts concerning an "objective basis for morality" (or some other philosophical parallel) as though moral experience is subjective until we find an objective "ground." It seems rather the opposite. Moral space just *is* the reality of our shared world and in both its whole and its particulars, it echoes a divine original. And this can be shown![14] It is precisely the *public* nature of our claims that tests their strength and demonstrates their resilience.

For all the ways in which subjective states might render a thing plausible or implausible—we are still fundamentally in a *shared* reality, a *shared* world, a *shared* space in which we are all trying to make our way, and with at least *some* shared grounds upon which we can try to persuade one another. And it is in *this very real shared space*

[13] This was the title of a book he published in 1962.

[14] A helpful discussion can be found in Tim Keller, *Making Sense of God: An Invitation to the Skeptical* (New York: Viking, 2016), 176-92. This is made sense of, however, within a philosophy of being which moves from ordinary experience in its multifaceted dimensions to see the structures of reality more broadly (never entertaining Hume's fact/value distinction). For an especially accessible philosophy of being along these lines, see Peirre-Marie Emonet, *The Dearest Freshness Deep Down Things: An Introduction to the Philosophy of Being* (New York: Herder & Herder, 1999). For an application of this approach, see Joe Puckett's wonderful *The Apologetics of Joy: A Case for the Existence of God from C.S. Lewis's Argument from Desire* (Eugene: Wipf & Stock, 2012).

that Christ really came and stood in front of people's actual faces. It is into *this shared space* that He rose from the dead. And it in *this shared space, in reality*, real, hard-core, brass-tacks, concrete, steel, blood, sweat, tears, and pain reality that we can still confidently proclaim that Jesus is the risen Lord of this world. And for precisely this reason, it is also in this very *public* shared space that these shared struggles which we are attempting to elucidate can be ministered to by Him.

Let me be extremely clear that I am speaking here about public persuasion concerning truth-claims as such. I am not speaking of the human heart or conversion, which ultimately has to do with an "evaluation" of truth claims that goes beyond their mere truth. Again, the demons believe that God is one, but their evaluation of this makes them shudder. Changing this deeper evaluation is ultimately a work of the Spirit. While it ordinarily attends persuasion concerning the truths themselves (and therefore renders our attempts at persuasion evangelistic), intellectual persuasion and proper evaluation that these truths obtain, that they are good, and that they are good *for me*—are, in principle, separate things

MOVING TOWARD AN ALTERNATIVE

In any case, how then do we respond to and speak into our common situation? Anticipating the next two chapters, I want to consider two questions. In chapter two, I will try to explain both why I think the existence of God can be proven and why I think atheism can still *seem* persuasive. Why is that? It is because our tacit sense of reality has been shaped (though not entirely so, and this is important) by modern technological culture. To unpack this claim, I will ask, "What does the modern technological order suggest about what it means for a thing to be real?" I think that if we ask and answer this question, we will significantly deflate (but not totally eradicate) our own temptations toward atheism.

And so, in chapter three, I will reflect upon the fact that we are, nevertheless, here after all. We are where we are, and the question becomes what our calling is in precisely this ideological context. Since I have argued that this temptation is a radically contingent one and highly related to our particular historical moment and culture, there is some question concerning whether or not we can even do anything about this in the first place. One popular option is to say we should "get back" or "get forward" to a world that is more like the middle ages, at least in this respect. I am going to argue, by contrast, that the modern situation (despite our temptation to atheism) is actually an improved situation for the modern believer rather than a hindrance. And the question which I hope will open this up for us is the following: "How interested is God in people merely believing in His existence?" I believe that asking and answering this question brings us quickly into distinctively Christian territory and a uniquely Christian perspective on human faith and freedom.

III:

THE SILENCING OF GOD

WHAT I AIM to do in the current chapter, as previously promised, is to explain why it is that someone can both find atheism philosophically and intellectually incoherent and yet still find himself attracted to it as a plausible conception of reality. In my judgment, to capture why this is so necessitates looking carefully at modern attitudes towards science, the relationship between science and technology, as well as the relationship of both science and technology to the plausibility of religious claims (or their alternative). Though the relevance of these things might seem obvious, I beg your patience if the relevance is not immediately clear to you. While my ultimate goal is to get at how it is that atheism can have an intellectual pull even on those who find it incoherent, I don't think we can do this without trying to understand why it is that atheists conceive of themselves as being reasonable in being atheists and why theists conceive of themselves as reasonable in being theists. In much of the recent discussion, this conversation has tended to focus on the relative value of the concrete sciences vs. the relative value of comparatively speculative and abstract philosophy.

And so I conceive of the present chapter as an intervention into a discussion, broadly speaking, between those who believe that the scientific method has materialist or naturalist implications, and those who believe that science cannot, even in principle, address matters traditionally labeled "metaphysical." Let us call them "materialists" and "metaphysicians" (though there are problems with both terms) as a problematic first approximation—though we will nuance this below. And let it be noted here that by "scientific method," one might be emphasizing some set of rules or, more broadly, a certain intellectual or *set of* intellectual values. In any case, for the metaphysicians, the materialist group appears to be frustratingly obstinate when it comes to the question of ontology—even as they (so it is argued) unwittingly play the parasite on irreducibly philosophical premises. To the materialists, the metaphysicians appear to play with words concerning abstract objects about which human beings have no good reason to confidently speculate. Or, put more simply, materialists believe that the emperor of metaphysics has no clothes while metaphysicians argue that that materialists only *perceive* the emperor to be naked because they wear philosophical *x-ray glasses* unawares.

My intervention in several steps: First, I want to summarize a fairly common naturalist viewpoint concerning causality. What is causality and why might it have materialist implications? And note, I'm treating naturalism and materialism together here for reasons I will explain in a moment. But suffice it to say that I'm trying to capture broad phenomena and general intellectual tendencies which admit of plenty of exceptions. So please don't think I intend to speak for all atheists, though I hope to speak for many or most of them. Second, I will briefly detail the philosophical and historical responses to this view, as well as why I don't think they sufficiently address what makes materialist claims "feel" plausible in the first place—even to those who reject them. Third, then, I will argue that this tension is explained by certain features of the modern technological order (defined in temporal terms as the post-Industrial cultural order increasingly dominated by machines and their "concerns," and in cognitive terms as that order in which technical modes of thought are tacitly perceived as having a unique ability to access and therefore to define reality). If this seems confusing for the present, I think it will become clear soon. I will conclude that this analysis has a deflationary effect on the materialist posture toward metaphysics.

glorified machines and so we glorify being like machines

CAUSALITY AND ATHEISM

For those who argue that modern science has materialist or ontologically naturalist implications, it is often thought that identifying (by direct observation or by inference) a regular sequence of events in the material world which terminate in a phenomenon constitutes a sufficient causal explanation of that phenomenon. Again, "science" here could be understood as a set of principles or as a sort of epistemic value-structure, but the above applies to both. I have mentioned two elements: a regular sequence and observability. I would not deny that someone might identify more features—albeit, I suspect, with the same import. By "regular sequence," I mean the repeatable and predictable correlation of one event with another. The "sequence" aspect is important because it is normally assumed that the prior event in a sequence sufficiently explains the appearance of the subsequent event. One modern field, for instance, in which the emphasis on sequence is particularly prominent is that of cognitive neuroscience. It is commonly supposed that if one can identify a regular brain-event (say, the lighting of a certain brain area in an MRI scan) which is apparently prior to a correlated mind-event (say, the subject, the person, undergoing the MRI indicating when they are conscious of an experience), that we can conclude that the brain-event is a sufficient explanation of the mind-event. And this example highlights, as well, the meaning of "observability" in these sequences. We do not, for example, see atoms directly, but they can be "observed" through a medium (in the above case, an MRI machine) which records their impact. Involved in this type of observation is normally our ability to predict the effects of a thing materially, and (in principle, but not always in fact) to interfere with, manipulate, shape, and redirect them. This is because the thing under consideration manifests itself in the realm of the material—and material is in principle manipulable and capable of being interfered with. Perhaps another way to say this is that these regular sequences must be publicly verifiable events which commonly confront the human senses (sometimes through a medium), yet manifest themselves as part of the order of things over which human beings can in principle exercise increasing degrees of control.

Now, why might this construal of "sufficient explanation" (that is, observable sequences in the realm in which humans can, in principle, interfere) have materialist implications? Daniel Dennett is one proponent of this position, and his masterful *Darwin's Dangerous Idea* is an intoxicating argument for the naturalist viewpoint.[1] Darwin, argues Dennett, has provided us with an idea, a "universal acid," which threatens to eat through all of our intuitions. To wit, all the apparent complexity of nature might be the outcome of a basic algorithmic property (a very simple rule of sorting what does and what does not happen) in physical sequence after physical sequence. And for Dennett, this model, especially as it is able to dig deeper and deeper and explain more and more, seems to increasingly explain all of the phenomena we encounter— leaving us with no need to reference anything beyond the material realm. He does not, of course, argue that we *have* explained everything. He argues, rather, that there is no phenomenon of which we are aware that has *refused* an explanation in materialist terms. And so, by implication, sequences of (in principle) observable events, operating on extremely basic underlying rules, account for all that we see. It was difficult to imagine this before Darwin, but when he introduced the possibility that complexity could arise out of a relatively mindless process, it rendered plausible the notion that a "mindless process" (a purely material sequence) is all that there is. Dennett uses the helpful analogy of skyhooks and cranes. The construction of all that we see before us does not require suspension in anything outside of our realm of awareness (e.g. like a building construction project performed by a skyhook whose "foundation" we cannot see in the sky). Rather, each design is suspended atop something very simple—

---

[1] Daniel Dennett, *Darwin's Dangerous Idea* (New York: Simon & Schuster, 1996).

even as it interacts with the world and creates even greater complexity (i.e. like a crane constructing a building whilst itself sitting atop the very same ground *as* the building). Human beings, for instance, are the product of an enormous number of physical, chemical, and biological cranes that have coalesced from simple beginnings to the complex outcome of nature's construction project which we call the human being. But no reference to skyhooks is needed to account for the building of this organism.

Physicist Victor Stenger, as well, argues that the trajectory of anything meaningfully called "science" throughout its history tends toward materialism. His recent *God and the Folly of Faith* is largely a survey of the history of science in its relationship to philosophy, metaphysics, and religion.[2] In this survey, he argues that concrete observations have continually falsified theses built atop a foundation of philosophical or religious speculation. And over time, science has been so successful that there is very little explanatory space left for undetectable agencies or any other imaginary placeholder for fine-grained empirical evidence. Stenger's narrative is a particularly prominent exhibit of what Charles Taylor has recently called a "subtraction story" concerning the advent of modern materialism.[3] That is, modern materialism and/or a-religion is basically a function of "taking away" (bit by bit) anything but material postulates such that all that is "left over" is predictable and relatively manipulable material.

Even Nancy Cartwright, who has perhaps done more than any other modern philosopher of science to lend

---

[2] Victor Stenger, *God and the Folly of Faith* (Amherst: Prometheus Press, 2012).

[3] See Charles Taylor, *A Secular Age*, 25-89.

credence to Aristotle's notions of "nature" and "powers" (typically considered to be immaterialist hypotheses), is nevertheless careful to note that she wishes to "replace occult powers by powers that are visible, though it may take a very fancy experiment to see them."[4] Note again that "observability" is a broad category. Materialist or (at least) naturalist explanation does not require direct observation, but only interaction with an entity in such a way that it manifests itself as belonging to the material world. That is, it is relatively predictable and belongs to an order of things with which the human can interfere. And the greater our tools, the less the world can resist us.

As an aside, Cartwright exhibits the instinct which underscores why I am treating "materialism" and "ontological naturalism" together. There are varieties, after all, of naturalists who are not, as such, materialists (say, property dualists who believe that material and mental properties are twin phenomenal progeny of the same noumenal parent). But these *technical* non-materialists nevertheless agree that our primary access-point to reality is via regular predictable sequences which are relatively (again, in principle) manipulable—that is, that technically immaterial properties nevertheless causally *belong*, for all practical purposes, to their material counterparts such that manipulation of the one is manipulation of the other. Consequently, there is little felt need to invoke anything outside of what can be described in this manner (such as Dennett's skyhooks or any sort of extra-material "agency") to explain the world before them, in general or in particular. For purposes of the specific question before us,

---

[4] Nancy Cartwright, *The Dappled World: A Study of the Boundaries of Science* (New York: Cambridge University Press, 1999), 80.

then, "materialism" and "naturalism" (at least as defined above) are only as distinct in their philosophical purchase as a minted dollar and a paper dollar backed by bullion.

One response to this view of causality is to agree with the starting point (that causes are identified through observing regular sequences in the physical world), but to argue that the final result of this starting point leads us beyond the material world. The proponents of Intelligent Design, for instance, basically accept the scientific starting points of observability and regular sequence, but then conclude that these necessarily terminate in their own inadequacy. That is, the material phenomena that we observe cannot be accounted for on an algorithmic model but necessarily require a "skyhook" as part of the explanation. They speak of what they call "irreducible complexity," that is the existence of certain physical phenomena which cannot (they say) reasonably be argued to be the outcome of a process. And so, they go on to invoke what their community has labeled a "design inference," which must obtain when materialist explanations simply will not do.[5] God, or something mind-like, is therefore seen as a sort of necessary explanation for things which cannot possibly be explained by an endless sequence of material events. "That is," retorts the materialist, "until they *can*."[6]

The critical response to this is that it is a "God of the gaps" argument. Intelligent Design proponents fill in gaps

---

[5] The godfather of this movement, William Dembski, coined the term in his work of the same title, *The Design Inference: Eliminating Chance Through Small Probabilities* (New York: Cambridge University Press, 1998).

[6] See Niall Shanks, *God, The Devil, and Darwin: A Critique of Intelligent Design Theory* (New York: Oxford University Press, 2004).

of human knowledge with a "just so" story of occult invisible powers. But this, it is argued, is to ground science in human ignorance rather than in a *positive* postulate that is inferred from the evidence itself. It is a failure of scientific imagination and patience. It is destructive to the scientific enterprise, which would here call for an admission of ignorance and a commitment to further investigation rather than to the sudden conclusion that "God" must be what fills in the causal gaps that we cannot fill. The point is not that the claim is demonstrably wrong, but that one cannot know that it is right because future work might yield explanations that we do not currently know or might not even be able to currently imagine! Stenger's book, mentioned above, is particularly helpful in showing precisely how this logic has failed over time. Throughout the history of natural philosophy, perceived gaps have been filled, one after the other, with models which explain material realities in a way that would have previously been inconceivable (and for which God was often invoked as the necessary explanation). This is why, for Dennett, Darwin is so important. It is not just that he presented new facts and theories, but that he had a scientific *imagination*. He imagined a different world, and the world yielded and continues to yield to his idea. Perhaps the greatest criticism that could be made of Intelligent Design, then, is that it stifles the scientific imagination. It is not that it is impossible. It is that it is lazy. Let us move then, secondly, to some typical philosophical (rather than scientific) and historical responses to modern materialism—both of which I take to be correct but also, as I will argue below, inadequate.

PHILOSOPHICAL AND HISTORICAL RETORT
Philosophical Retort

What is almost always missed, in these discussions, is the difference between the Intelligent Design response to materialism or ontological naturalism and the relatively broader function that God plays in late medieval and early modern metaphysics. For these philosophers, the explanation(s) of events in terms of materiality and in terms of divine agency were not *necessarily* (an important qualifier) in tension. Divine and natural agency were not of a common causal reservoir, such that if materiality accounted for a cause only 75%, then God accounted for it 25% or vice versa. Rather, there was an aspect of each event that answered 100% to "mind" and an aspect of each event that answered 100% to materiality. To this day, this is why there are many religious persons, especially among Roman Catholics, who are quite comfortable with Darwin's evolutionary theory (even comparatively strong forms of it) but who do not believe that scientific hypotheses can ever in principle get at the aspect of "causality" and "explanation" that is uniquely accounted for by God. To clarify, I do not mean to assume Darwinism here. That is a different discussion. I am simply arguing that, in principle, the following notion of causality and of the necessity of God within that notion would obtain whether or not Darwinism, as a biological hypothesis, is true.

Moving on. Essential to this non-reductionism of causal space, as these thinkers might prefer to speak of it, is the latter's appropriation of Aristotle's fourfold notion of causality—often identified as material, efficient, formal, and final causality. Each of these, so it is argued, constitute an aspect of the "total explanation" of a thing.[7] Materiality is the "stuff" within which an event is instantiated and observed. Efficient causality has to do with the ordered relation of one event to another—the sense in which a prior being causes a subsequent being. Note that this need not imply a temporal *before* and *after*. From one perspective, billiard ball *a* causing billiard ball *b* to move involves a temporal sequence. But classically speaking, the causal "event" itself is singular. The event of billiard ball *a* moving and of billiard ball *b* being moved is the same event from two perspectives. Nevertheless, there is a sort of sequentiality in their relationship that makes efficient causality that dimension of causality most fitted to analyzing temporal sequences in our experience—i.e. first I saw *a* hit *b*, and then I saw *b* go into the hole. These two aspects of causality, some argue, capture what is the "explanatory realm" of science. Science is concerned mainly with sequences in the material (i.e. observable) realm. But on this view, even if each event in the world had a material correlate and an efficient causality chain which went back infinitely, *in no individual case* (nor in all the cases of causality together) would this constitute the total explanation of any thing or all things. A total explanation also requires a "formal cause"—the "in virtue of what" one thing produces a certain sort of effect rather than another, or conversely, the "in virtue of what" a thing is effected in just this way rather than that way. This is that piece of the explanation of events that your child is fascinated by when he asks, perhaps to your annoyance,

---

[7] See the accessible treatment of Edward Feser, *The Last Superstition* (South Bend: St. Augustine Press, 2010), 27-73.

"why?" Why was the glass shattered? Because a brick was thrown at it. Why do bricks break glass rather than bounce off of it? Because glass is fragile and bricks are heavy and hard. Why does heaviness rather than lightness break fragile things? (Admittedly, this is a philosophical child.) Because of their chemical compositions. Well why can't this chemical composition have this effect rather than that? Etc.

Our imaginary medievals would simply tell their children that the "nature" of a thing, either in terms of its active powers to effect certain ends (say, the ability of hands to mold clay) or its passive powers to be effected toward certain ends (say, the ability of clay to be molded by hands) is part of the explanation of how an event unfolded as it did. Even if one reduces the "in virtue of what" a thing behaves as it does to its components (i.e. say water to its elements, its elements to particles, etc.), at some point one will presumably need to account for the "in virtue of what" a particular sort of thing, rather than another sort of thing, happens. For instance, even if all causal force reduced to the motions of a quantum field, one can still ask "in virtue of what" the field produces just these sorts of effects rather than others. One can imagine a possible universe in which a quantum field produces radically different effects (or even had a radically different range of options to effect). The question is, therefore, what it is about the quantum field that reduces its causal force to just the effects that it *does*, in fact, produce. Unlike we moderns, the medievals actually had a stopping point for that inquisitive (and sometimes annoying) child, and that stopping point was "because God willed it to be this way." Why did God will it to be this way? Because of His wise, holy, and loving will. Why did God's wise, holy, and loving will decide that it be this way? Because of His wise, holy, and loving will. This is not an explanatory throw-away, but rather that beyond which no answer is possible *by the very definition of what an answer is*—including the definition of that about which there can be an "answer" in the traditional sense.

Here we meet the much-maligned concept of "final causality." While formal causality is focused on the "what" that is producing an effect, final causality is focused on the "end" which the "what" produces. That is, things (in virtue of their natures) "tend toward" one end rather than another. And this is just to say that they act "as though" they have conscious "goals" toward x rather than toward y. Again, imagine a possible world in which a particular sort of event terminated in a radically different effect than it does in our world (say, that ice cream produced a strong sense of sourness). Given that it doesn't in *this world*, it is not difficult to imagine why, without our *modern* instincts, it might have been natural for our ancestors to think about sweetness, especially in its natural relation to its natural ends (note the relationship of naturally sweet things like fruit to energy and survival) as actually the more fundamental reality than the things which produce it. To attain the goal of just this kind of "sweetness" (which, in nature, itself has the goal of giving high amounts of energy), then, does not reduce to the other aspects of the total explanation of a thing producing the effect of sweetness. Rather, its primal and metaphysically prior mode of being (its sheer facticity) is that in lieu of which the what, how, and where of the other aspects of causality are as they are. The "what," "how," and "where," answer to the "why" at precisely the moment they are shown to be inseparable aspects of any explanation of being, and at the same time *not* reducible to one another. This will get us back to God in a moment. But let us try to understand this just a little bit more clearly.

Think of those human experiences to which we have the most certain access. Indeed, most of the time, the "final effect" is actually our first access point into understanding "what" a thing is. It is our portal into a "what" standing out in the community of beings as they commonly confront us.[8] For instance, we see a "hopping green thing." Certainly, it is "material," but our minds don't think "material" or merely "hoppingness" or "green," but we confront it as a phenomenal whole. "Whoa! Hopping green thing!" This phenomenal *peculiarity* sets it apart from other things and so we then decide to distinguish it from other critters as a "frog." This is what it is. Closer inspection and observation shows us a larger complex array of sequences of which this thing is regularly a part and out of which it "originates," (generation, environment, etc.). And it is actually here that its "materiality" becomes most manifest, composed as a frog is of many material parts with which we can (and with which many little mischievous children *do)* interfere. One way of saying this is that we are not confronted with "matter" when we are confronted with a frog. Indeed, a

---

[8] On this, see the incomparable treatment of metaphysics, articulated around the concept of a "community of beings," in W. Norris Clarke's *The One and the Many: A Contemporary Thomistic Metaphysics* (Notre Dame: University of Notre Dame Press, 2001). On the relation of such to physics, see Robert Spitzer, *New Proofs for the Existence of God: Contributions from Contemporary Physics and Philosophy* (Grand Rapids: Eerdmans, 2010).

better way of getting at this would be to say that we are never confronted with "matter" at all in the abstract. "Matter," in fact, does not exist—stand out—among beings. *Things* (like frogs) exist as a particular "mode" or "relative manifestation" of materiality, but our mind's first motion is actually to grasp the unique act of a thing, then consciously distinguish it from other things, examine *how* it is what it is, and then (perhaps) to interact with it via its materiality as such. Granted, all of this is manifest materially, necessary as our senses are to present a frog to the mind, but the point is that this manifestation cannot be abstracted from or conflated with its being manifest intellectually, consciously, understandingly, interpretively, relative to other things and aspects of reality. And while all these causes present themselves simultaneously, our actual grasp of the material aspect of its cause (i.e. how matter organizes to produce this thing) is later in our understanding and interaction *with* the thing—though we are aware *that* it is material immediately. Materiality answers to questions (what is it made out of, what does it feel like, how many gizzards does it have, what happens when I do this? How does materiality coalesce to produce just this thing?) which usually come later in our understanding of a thing's uniqueness, and its distinction from other things.

Because this is such an important point to communicate, I will try to get at it just one more way. Final causes are *metaphysically* but not *temporally* prior to the aspects of causality oriented toward a particular end. This is manifest to the extent that we can (once again) imagine the effects of *a* and *b* as producing *d* instead of *c*. Why do they produce *c*, however? It is not generally a matter of logical or metaphysical necessity. We can imagine coherent and different orders or arrangements of things. Rather, in the absolutely contingent order of things that populates and constitutes our experience, particular effects correspond to particular causes without being reducible to them. That is, the phenomenal whole is not reducible to the sum of its material, efficient, and formal parts. This "end" has its own coherent being as the prior goal toward which the other aspects of causality work according to an established and contingent relationship.[9]

In any case, this manner of thinking about causality and "explanation" was more or less the common sense of the medieval and early modern worlds, and despite famous criticisms, it remained influential for significant portions of the philosophical community until well into the 18th century. That is to say, this model survived, and many did not see it as in tension with the scientific method. But dependent as its plausibility, as an articulated philosophical postulate, was on its kindred philosophically ornate vocabulary and concepts, it tended to die wherever scholasticism (and my own historical hunch, the concept of divine simplicity) failed to exert influence, and it has perhaps all but perished in intellectual environments where nothing "invisible" seems plausible at all.

Nevertheless, interestingly, there has been a resurgence in recent philosophy of this non-reductive notion of causality. I have already mentioned Nancy Cartwright's re-invocation of "powers" and "natures"—

---

[9] It might be objected that I am assuming that conceivability implies metaphysical possibility—even if not actuality. For answer to objections concerning this (including the famous objections of Saul Kripke), see Edward Feser, *The Philosophy of Mind* (Oxford: OneWorld, 2006), 29-38.

though she is nervous about any "occult" (which is just a snarky way of saying "immaterial") definitions of these notions. It is difficult to imagine, however, how one could fully avoid some philosophically offensive sense of the "occult" (i.e. basically invisible vs. mechanical agency) in any meaningful definition of the "nature" of a thing or its "power" to produce certain effects. In order to make sure we grasp this and to make sure we see the relationship of all of this to the question of God, let's briefly expand the above discussion. One can imagine a world in which *thing 1* produces *effect 2* rather than *effect 1*. The question would then be, "Why doesn't *thing 1* produce *effect 1* rather than *effect 2* in this world?" And it would be difficult to answer this beyond saying, "Because it doesn't," or "Because of what it does and does not do in virtue of its 'nature.'" But then we have to ask why being *thing 1* or having the nature of *thing 1* is such that *effect 1* rather than *effect 2* is produced. And so on through an inferential chain. "Well, because of *thing 1*'s relationship to *meta-thing 1*!" So why did *meta-thing 1* produce *thing 1* rather than *thing 2,* and so on? At some point, it will be very difficult to avoid something very "occult"-like, some explanation that goes, "Because that's just the way things are!" Again, even if all causality reduced back to a quantum field of some sort, the question would then be why the quantum field produces "this" rather than "that" when it is possible to imagine a world in which it did (even radically) otherwise. In short, it does not seem to be a sufficient "explanation" of its own effects because there are still more basic realities (*possible* beings which do not obtain, existence itself, etc.) which are left out of the equation and ultimately unrelated to what *actually* exists. In other words, that annoying kid who keeps asking "why" could one-up you on this one. This is why the scholastics' "first cause" is not the first domino in a causal series, kick-starting the great chain reaction of history. Indeed, Aquinas did not think you could refute an infinite series of causes in temporal succession, and yet he still thinks in terms of a "first cause" metaphysically. Rather, the "first" in "first cause" is a metaphysical "first," the "ground of being," or "existence itself," or "being qua being"—which suspends all possible and actual beings in itself, and which therefore is not "a being" about which existence or non-existence can even be predicated. Rather, properly understood, such a "first cause" is that without which there is no explanation for any particular (possible or actual) beings at all.

In my judgment, this is inescapable. The cosmos is irreducibly particular. There are no forces, nor can we imagine materially-related forces, which are metaphysically or rationally necessary such that their non-existence would entail something like incoherence. But we *can* say this of the act of existence itself (Kant's objections notwithstanding). To imagine the non-existence of being itself, of existence itself, of "isness" in the most basic sense, is arguably to speak nonsense. In this very basic insight is the distinction between necessary being and contingent being. The former is purely actual, what and as it is—the contrary of which is incoherence. The latter can rationally be conceived of as not being, the contrary being completely rational, and therefore demonstrates itself to be, while actual in fact, only potential and non-necessary in principle. This is hugely important. *Even if a contingent thing has always existed in time, and even if there is a massive multiverse, it is still a multiverse which is not absolutely metaphysically necessary at the cost of incoherence*, and its eternal existence means nothing except that something which "need not, as such, be at all" has *come into being* temporally. Likewise, a thing might not have come into being temporally but might still be metaphysically contingent and non-absolute and non-necessary. And this still leaves the question of what accounts for it at all (even if it had no temporal beginning). This is the difference between the traditional definition of God and the being of the created order. There is necessarily some "pure actuality" which just "is." The incoherence of atheism is that it declares the contingent "purely actual," and it metaphysically stops at a non-necessary and "could meaningfully have been otherwise" entity—which then has no explanation for *why* it is this sort of thing rather than another, *why* this possibility is actualized, even *why* this multiverse is eternally actualized rather than some other multiverse. And if the multiverse or quantum field does not exist by some metaphysical necessity, and yet we say that it is the most basic reality, then we have effectively violated the law of causality—saying that something which does not have existence by definition nevertheless just does exist without explanation. Of course, some take the bait—but only at the cost of a deep and foundational incoherence. This is not so with theism. God is the I AM. He is being, necessary being, the denial of which/whom is incoherent. God is not, in other words, does not just "happen to be" actual within a "possibility space" of other alternatives. He is the very ground of possibility (itself a finite category). In respect of being and existence, it is contingency and finitude which are the great mystery (God Himself being simply necessary). And this, then, explains precisely why the universe is what and is it is, why gravity could have been 9.87 meters/second squared but is rather 9.86 meters/second square 1. To wit, if a thing does not have its being in itself, it mu t have it in another. If it does not have its being by n cessity, it must have its being in contingency. And w at sort of reality bridges the gap between contingent beings which only "might be" in principle and contir gent beings which "are" in fact? Ultimately, it must e a matter of agency, of will, of personhood—the wa an artist makes a single thing out of infinite possibilities. The alternative is to say that contingent things are made necessary by other contingent things, and those by other contingent things, and so on. But if all things in ou cosmos are precisely as they appear to us (necessarily ontingent and could have been otherwise), then this eaves this entire chain *(eternal or not)* suspended in mere contingency. Something must still bridge the gap between "might have been otherwise" realities and "what a tually is" reality. And, indeed, it is worse than that. *This s not just true of the chain as a whole, but of each link within the ain—each link being a "could have been otherwise" effect of its pre ecessor.* The implication of this is that the marks of agenc and will do not depend upon "irreducible comple ty" or some other such notion. Agency, will, personl ood, and art are necessarily manifest at every step of the c usal chain because every step could have been otherwise —and this is true whether we are looking at a human ye or a single particle. The whole chain *and* each of i links are suspended in mind-like directedness—having this rather than that nature and performing this act ra her than that one.

I realize this is all very dense, but I think that the basic insight here can be grasped by a child. Medieval children could ask "why" and their Thomist priests could gleefully tell them about "pure actuality," the terminus point of the why for any finite thing—itself necessarily existing and its will (because it's will/wisdom/love) accounting for things which could have been otherwise existing. The gap between what must exist and what does but need not exist is necessarily mediated by a non-necessary donation from what necessarily exists, and that requires will and personality. Our act of existence is suspended in and is a donation of Existence Himself—Being Himself, Life Himself—in whom all things hold and are what and as they are—from whom are all things, for whom are all things, and in whom all things hold together.

Now, much more could be said. I could develop other arguments that might give someone a reason to believe in God. I could modify this argument, consider other features of being (mind, love, beauty, etc.) that are necessarily interchangeable with our word "being" when we talk about God.[10] But, in short, the reason why someone might still believe in God is because it is incoherent not to. So much for the philosophical response to materialism. What of the historical response?

Historical Retort

Another response to materialism, for those who want to recover Aristotle's more metaphysically robust notion of

---

[10] On the "transcendentals," as Thomist philosophers call them, see W. Norris Clarke, *The One and the Many*, 290-302.

causality, is historic l in nature. Why, after all, did Aristotle's arguments lecline in influence in the first place? Did someone philos iphically "refute" him? Obviously, certain aspects of A stotelian physics were falsified, but his metaphysics are q ite extractable from this. Again, it is for this reason tha many who are Aristotelians on causality are not pa ticularly nervous about Darwinian evolution, physical "t eories of everything," and so forth. At best, such theorie are only theories of "everything" in the realm of materi l and efficient causality—but they cannot even in princi le get at formal and final causality— which are part of the otal explanation of a thing.

In any case, the nistorical argument admits of both a negative and a positi e inflection. Negatively, one way to make the case is to show that, for instance, Darwin's recipients among the religious were not always nervous about the theologi al implications of his theory.[11] Positively, another w y is to reveal the tenuous historical and philosophical c cumstances in which Aristotelian philosophy was ori inally critiqued and progressively dismissed. Whether d e to the influence of the mechanistic model of the unive se, the influence of late medieval nominalism, or to t e critique of scholasticism's often bemusing mental acr batics ("How many angels can dance on the head of a in," etc.), the argument of many historians is that Ar totle was not so much refuted as philosophically fired. Speaking concerning the demise of

[11] See David N. Livingsto ne, *Darwin's Forgotten Defenders: The Encounter Between Evangelical Theology and Evolutionary Thought* (Vancouver: Regent College Publishing, 1984).

[12] The classic treatment re ains E.A. Burtt's *The Metaphysical Foundations of Modern Science* (Mineola: over, 1932).

Aristotle in relation to Galileo, for example, Paul Feyerabend writes that,

> It is clear that allegiance to the new ideas will have to be brought about by means other than arguments.... The barbaric Latin spoken by the scholars, the intellectual squalor of the academic science, its other-worldliness which is soon interpreted as uselessness, its connection with the Church—all these elements are now lumped together with the Aristotelian cosmology, and the contempt one feels for them is transferred to every single Aristotelian argument.[13]

On this view, the firing of Aristotle may have been understandable, but it was not philosophical, and any sense that subsequent scientific development since the early modern era "refutes" Aristotle is rooted in a historical amnesia concerning what the scholastics actually believed. Our judgment that his is not a live philosophical option is more a historical accident than the result of a truly *critical* evaluation.[14]

The Inadequacy of the Retorts

And so, we have before us a philosophical and a historical response to the current "live option" of ontological naturalism. In my judgment, these responses are helpful,

---

[13] Paul Feyerabend, *Against Method* (New York: Verso, 2010), 113-4.

[14] On this, see Etienne Gilson's *From Aristotle to Darwin and Back Again: A Journey in Final Causality, Species, and Evolution* (Notre Dame: Ignatius Press, 2009).

but by themselves, will usually be unpersuasive. One cannot help but get the sense that there has been little advance in this debate on either side, despite the fact that the substantive arguments have not really changed. The materialists, having the *ethos* of a confident younger generation which dismisses its elders, often portray the metaphysicians as anti-progressive, dogmatic, full of linguistic speculation and *gobbledygook*—and therefore as unworthy of engagement. And the metaphysicians, having the *ethos* of grandparents who grumble about "kids these days," tend to private insecurity (hopefully somewhat explained in a moment) and to a public dismissal of the materialists as juvenile.

For the sake of persuasion, the above arguments need supplementation with an account of why the materialist option is felt to be plausible in the first place. Why does it, for many, seem like the intellectual default position? And perhaps most illuminating, why do its hypotheses and its mistrust of philosophy resonate, in many instances, even with its critics? Who does not feel the sting of the Enlightenment witticisms at the expense of scholasticism, its critique of system-building and speculation, and its orientation to concrete realities which often win arguments simply because, once *observed* and *understood* (very important qualifiers), a person's will is normally powerless to disbelieve what is manifestly in front of their face?[15] There appears to be a plausibility structure which is shared by

---

[15] To get a sense of the power of the Enlightenment critique, one must peruse Peter Gay's *The Enlightenment: The Rise of Modern Paganism* (New York: Norton, 1966).

those who affirm and those who deny this option, and the question is what this is.[16]

Similar analysis can extend to the historical argument as well. Arguing that Aristotle was never really refuted does not account for why alternative hypotheses were initially deemed plausible. Nor should we think that religion itself was at stake in the original debate. Almost all the critics of Aristotelianism and Thomism were themselves Christians and theists! The shift away from this required other, and very complicated, historical and ideological steps. Furthermore, even if Aristotelian metaphysics have philosophical plausibility, it is not necessarily true that they were ultimately believed for philosophical reasons in the early modern period—even among the scholastics. We need to account for the fact that many abandoned Aristotelian philosophy for precisely the reasons that its modern defenders say one need not do so.[17] The Feyerabend quote above is a case in point. It is really *modern* persons who more easily distinguish the debate concerning Intelligent Design and the debate over God as the ground of being. It is *we* who more easily have our Aristotelianism and our heliocentrism at the same time. That is to say, we can cope with the possibility of holding to one position without the other because these ideas do not initially confront us as requiring one another. They are disaggregated in our intellectual experience. Another way of saying this is that the "purchase" of final

---

[16] On modern plausibility structures, see (again) Taylor's *A Secular Age*, esp. 362, 555, 562-63.

[17] On this and the above, see Stephen Gaukroger, *The Emergence of a Scientific Culture: Science and the Shaping of Modernity 1210-1685* (New York: Oxford University Press, 2006).

causality in our context is highly abstract, if it has purchase for any of us at all. But for medieval persons, its most prominent icons were agencies that suffused the cosmos and which were, more often than not, felt to be right in front of one's face. This is what many historians and sociologists refer to as the "enchanted world" of medieval Europe. What are the prominent examples of "mind-like agency and goal directedness" in the universe? It is angels and demons and fairies and saints and sacraments. And even plants and stars really "felt" like agents "doing" things. Though the latter were comparatively predictable, the primary reality was freedom and agency and "mind" and "will," the regularity of the planets being but a rigid form of this. Indeed, Christian faithfulness might be to "behave like the planets," which obey the natural law without fail. They're consistent! The universe was a chorus of communicators rather than an amalgam of machine parts.[18] Where does this leave us? How do we explain where *we* are at?

ATHEISM, MODERN TECHNO-CULTURE, AND "REALITY"

It is often suggested that this enchantment changed when human beings were able to "predict" the alleged "agencies" of the cosmos. I don't think this is quite a sufficient move. Regular prediction might shift one's perception of just how "rigid" particular modes of agency were, but the perception was still that natures "communicated" by acting. Furthermore, medieval natural

---

[18] On the medieval "world," see C.S. Lewis, *The Discarded Image* (New York: Cambridge University Press, 2012).

philosophers were constantly trying to predict the course of nature, and even to influence the activities of angels and demons—rendering *them* predictable.[19] And so, alternatively, I would argue that the real key to the progressive change and sense of things that has shifted in the West in the last 500 years is a change in the human ability to *control* these alleged agencies, rather than just to predict them. If a person is not only able to understand a thing, but to use it for his own ends, that same thing might increasingly be perceived less like an agent to which one is reciprocally subject (as agent to agent), than like a tool which is rather *entirely* subject to that person's agency and ends. And here we see a significant shift in the human's immediate practical "sense of things." As the modern era progressed, droughts which were formerly signs of divine judgment were now possible to control because of one's tools. Indeed, in our day, it is now normal to even *seek out* the desert for aesthetic purposes. Death was felt to be less and less a threat (through medicine, infrastructure, etc.) and comfort and distance from nature a more ubiquitous and extensive given. The philosophical waters were made even more murky when ecclesiastical invocations of divine judgment for increasing philosophical blasphemies or for the exploitation of nature went unrealized. This rendered even the (presumably) most agentic aspects of the cosmos effectively silent and invisible. The real story here, then, is the story of modern technological culture and its implicit postures toward "the real."

I will proceed from the concrete to the abstract. First, I will detail several *prima facie* reasons for considering the

---

[19] See David Lindberg, *The Beginnings of Western Science* (Chicago: University of Chicago Press, 2008).

correlation between enhanced technology and the plausibility of materialism (whether in its explicit philosophical variant or in its tacitly imbibed practical analogue), and I will then try to articulate what it is about modern technology which, in principle, can be interpreted as having a *causal* effect on the plausibility of materialism. Taking up "correlation" first, there are several items worth considering:

1. Modern technology is the most obvious and prominent payoff of the scientific method. Indeed, some have argued that there is less difference between the two than we are typically prone to think.[20] But the tumultuous relationship between science and metaphysics starts at about the advent of what we call the "scientific method." While not without precedent, Francis Bacon is fascinating for his massive influence on the development of the modern scientific method, which he specifically opposed to the methods and views of Aristotle. Bacon's method was self-consciously technological in focus (i.e. it attempted to control nature) *and* self-consciously anti-teleological.[21]

2. Furthermore, while certain scientific theories have changed, and while certain cosmologies have changed (indeed, drastically so) what has not ceased to progress is humans' ability to control their world. Arguably, there has been more control over the natural world gained in the last

---

[20] For different reflections upon this, see Lewis Mumford, "Science as Technology," *American Philosophical Society* 105.5 (1961): 506-11; Srdjan Lelas, "Science as Technology," *The British Journal for the Philosophy of Science* 44.3 (1993): 423-42; David Channell, *A History of Technoscience: Erasing the Boundaries Between Science and Technology* (New York: Routledge, 2017).

[21] See Steven Shapin, *The Scientific Revolution* (Chicago: The University of Chicago Press, 1998), 65-118.

500 years than in all of human history before this time put together. Alongside this trend has flourished ontological naturalism (See point 3). This could be a loose correlation, but arguably, the more specific correlation of materialism to major technological shifts implies the connection to be more tight than loose. To wit,

3. A. It is not until the Enlightenment *philosophes* that one detects a sizable number of materialists among the European intelligentsia. But this also happens to be an era of massive technological advancement. Indeed, many of the *philosophes* felt themselves to be living in the dawn of a new era, not just politically, but religiously and technologically. They were experiencing the "first-fruits" of the scientific method, the payoff that proved its unique claim to contact with reality.[22] B. Materialism remained a minority position among the elite, especially in England and America, until its popularization in the middle to the late 19th century. And in the realm of technology, this was the era of the Industrial Revolution, which was arguably a far more significant factor in the decline of religion in the late 19th and early 20th centuries than was Darwinism.[23] C. The next great leap in modern materialism was in the 1960's in the West, when materialism became a "live option" for the common man. At least in America, this was highly correlated with the height of the American middle-class as well as well as perhaps the greatest era of American world leadership in the realm of technological advancement.[24]

---

[22] See both the aforementioned and following volume by Peter Gay, *The Enlightenment: The Science of Freedom* (New York: Norton, 1969).

[23] See Charles Taylor, *A Secular Age*, 299-419.

[24] See Charles Taylor, *A Secular Age*, 423-535.

4. And even now, it is significant to note that irreligion is highly correlated with a materially comfortable lifestyle. That is, it is mostly a white, well-to-do phenomenon, which is to say that it is a phenomenon tied to a maximal state of self-agency and freedom.[25] Conversely, one will find very little irreligion among the developing world or *even among the poor in Western nations.* A common explanation of this is that such persons need a "crutch" of cosmic comfort, whereas the already comfortable, needing no such aid, are less motivated to consider the divine. This is, of course, the alter-ego of psychological reductionism along the lines of, "People are atheists just so they can do whatever they want."

So, these are brief observations which suggest a *correlation* between modern technology and the evaporation of the felt plausibility of traditional metaphysics. But what might be the actual *causal* feature in technology be? The features of modern technology which support these "bulwarks of (un)belief" (to bastardize a phrase from Charles Taylor) are, perhaps, obvious, but it is worth exploring several dimensions of the modern technological order explicitly:[26]

1. Bound up with the early modern abandonment of an Aristotelian definition of "nature" was a new relationship to that nature, such that it was perceived to be nature "for me" rather than an order of agencies to which I was subject. One can make too much of this, and it is important not to give into historically idealist temptations,

---

[25] See Phil Zuckerman, "Atheism, Secularity, and Well-being: How the Findings of Social Science Counter Negative Stereotypes and Assumptions," *Sociology Compass* 3.6 (2009): 949-71.

[26] The title of his first chapter in *A Secular Age* is "Bulwarks of Belief."

but it is not particularly controversial to note a relatively simultaneous shifting posture toward nature as "raw material" for human purposes and of nature as less a collection of "things" than a pile of matter subject to "laws." That is to say, the way we begin to even speak about nature is such that it is passive and inert, moved by laws outside of itself. And so human control could be realized inasmuch as that relationship could be harnessed for human ends. So, the world does not *communicate itself* to my senses, but rather my senses are active, and the world is an object I shape. *Inasmuch as this relationship to nature yielded the fruits of technological advancement and of knowledge, that initial posture seems reality-revealing.* That is to say, nature has yielded to what Taylor calls the "instrumental stance" toward itself.[27] It has subjected itself to man and given its fruits. And sensing that we have tapped into reality by construing our relationship with nature in this manner, our psyche might easily interpret its itch for reality *in general* to have been scratched rather than to have been (in some important respects) *numbed.* And so,

2. This relationship to nature, of course, was not absolute. But the continued holding of this posture and the increased proliferation of this posture's technological fruits cannot but have had a massive effect on the Western sense of what it means for a thing to be "real" at all. Different authors identify different points of technological development as particularly significant in this regard. Lewis Mumford is interested in modern mining.[28] Jacques Ellul is

---

[27] Charles Taylor, *A Secular Age*, 90-158.

[28] Lewis Mumford, *Technics and Civilization* (Chicago The University of Chicago Press, 1963), 60-106. Here he discusses "agents of mechanization."

less interested in locating particular points in the development of "the machine," but rather in the idea of "technique" itself.[29] Neil Postman points to the influence of early 20th century management principles (i.e. "Taylorism").[30] Martin Heidegger is fascinated by the difference between technologies which develop the inner potencies of nature and those which impose human ends upon nature artificially.[31]

Whatever the case, each of these authors is arguably trying to capture the way in which our posture toward nature, *which is itself reinforced by the technologies which mediate that relation* (that is a major point!), ultimately shapes our "imagination" concerning the real. Putting this differently, one might ask the following: *What does the modern technological order, and the relationship to nature that it mediates to us, suggest about what it means for a thing to be "real"?* In case it needs to be highlighted, this is the central question of this chapter and I think the hinge upon which my whole argument turns. The modern technological order tacitly communicates to us, day in and day out, that reality (the sort that actually concerns us), belongs to the order of the manipulable, that it is subject, in principle, to human agency. Each of the authors above, in his own way, contributes to this analysis. For Heidegger, modern technology is the "destining of revealing" such that nature "answers back" to me in the shape of my questions (i.e.

---

[29] Jacques Ellul, *The Technological Society* (New York: Vintage, 1967), esp. 13-19 for a discussion of definitions of technique.

[30] Neil Postman, *Technopoly: The Surrender of Culture to Technology* (New York: Vintage, 1993), 40-55.

[31] Martin Heidegger, "The Question Concerning Technology," in *Basic Writings*, ed. David Krell (New York: Harper, 2008), 307-42.

uses) for it. That reality seems like the kind of thing that we engage in our material manipulations has everything to do with how we have approached reality in the first place. For Ellul, "technique" is a pattern of thought which changes everything it touches, a reduction of reality to the terms of the instrumentally rational and ordered and the efficient. What does not fit this mold is ultimately "invisible."[32] Mumford and Postman are particularly concerned with this "invisibility." It is not that there is no longer a philosophical argument for "invisible" realities, but it is that we have been shaped to relate to the cosmos *practically* and therefore to *imagine* and be concerned with the cosmos only in its visible dimensions, or with that dimension with which human agency can, in principle, interfere. As such, any aspect of reality which does not manifest itself as "visible," as part of the realm of the manipulable, is perceived to be non-existent ("that with which we do not have to do"). Or, stated differently, the material and efficient realms are the only realms of concern and care for us. And so they alone are felt to exist, and scientific discourse is, then, tacitly perceived to "explain" reality without remainder–trafficking as it does in the realm(s) of material and efficient causality. Inasmuch, then, as materiality is *practically* that "as which" we perceive the real, it is natural for us to feel as though anything else is superfluous.

3. This account further helps to explain, again, why it is that a certain aversion to metaphysics is particularly prominent in well-to-do eras and nations. It is here that one can move around in a world that has been

---

[32] Jacques Ellul, *The Technological Society*, esp. 19-21.

"controlled" for the human and for whom, therefore, speculative and "unpractical" (that is, immediately unpractical) questions are simply irrelevant. I, for instance, live in an air-conditioned house. When a storm comes that would have been a crisis to my ancestors, I don't even flinch. I can hardly imagine what it is like to get food or water anywhere but a grocery store or a tap, the products of each appearing, for all practical purposes, as by magic (albeit I assume of the de-mystified technical sort in the hands of an anonymous, different sort of clergy). When I experience "nature," it is manicured nature, whether it be the neatly placed trees in my neighborhood, the mowed lawn, the pruned bushes, or the non-threatening sky. When I walk outside to the bus, the notion that my path is lit, that I walk on smooth concrete, that I am in a vehicle which transports me at high and efficient speeds, doesn't even enter my consciousness. This is "reality" to me. I *know* that it is technologically mediated, but only when I'm thinking about it. When I'm simply moving around in it, it is simply "the world." One could go on to speak of technologically mediated encounters with health, death, and other persons. Even those things, the most agentic aspects of reality (human relationships) are increasingly subjected to media, surrogates, and "options" which are historically unprecedented and mechanistic.[33] To put it bluntly, *the world* is a "world for me." I do not find myself in a big, mysterious world suffused with agencies to which I am subject and around which I must learn to navigate. I find myself in a world almost entirely tool-i-fied, a world

---

[33] See Nicholas Carr, *The Shallows: What the Internet is Doing to Our Brains* (New York: Norton, 2011).

of my own subjective agency before an increasingly silent cosmos. And a silent cosmos echoes no ultimate Speaker.

4. Of course, I live in a bubble, but it is an expanding bubble. My argument would suggest that the status of Western metaphysical beliefs will be largely dependent upon what happens to this bubble. Many, though by no means all, post-humanist or trans-humanist futures are religionless ones.[34] Increasingly, the traditional arguments of metaphysics are rendered dismissible by being rendered forgettable (because invisible, not immediate, impractical). The more we are able to move around in the world, to relate to other persons, to have and maintain social institutions, and to find personal fulfillment without reference to them—the more metaphysical claims seem implausible to us—the more philosophical (as opposed to concretely practical) reflection seems pointless. The inverse of this is that religion is likely to flourish where control over nature is at its least. This is not because persons with less control over nature need a crutch, but because reflecting upon and considering "the invisible" as real seems a plausible move to those who experience the world as something to which they are subject, as a powerful set of forces outside of them which they cannot harness. Indeed, in the perhaps distinctively late modern genre of dystopian fiction, even in the works of those authors who are explicitly atheists, it is interesting to note how often the question of God becomes relevant.[35] And even where metaphysical questions are not engaged

---

[34] See, for instance, Ray Kurzweil, *The Age of Spiritual Machines: When Computers Exceed Human Intelligence* (New York: Penguin Books, 2000).

[35] There is an interesting "God-hauntedness" in sci-fi of Cixin Liu and in the disaster novels of J.G. Ballard.

directly, much of this fiction has a sort of haunted quality, a re-enchantment of the cosmos in the smaller sense that it is once again rendered mysterious, quasi-agentic, a force outside of me to which I am ultimately subject. This is largely because in such stories, man's technical control of the world is taken away in a crisis. Man's sense of "how the world fits together" is completely shattered. His world of concern is not what it was. I would argue that, even now, there are two basic features of reality which often result in a massive shift in religious perspective. These are confrontations with "death" and confrontations with other persons when those persons "hurt" or "love" us. Love and death confront us as personal forces (though death might also be called anti-personal), extremely difficult to harness, disorientating facets of reality which are not easily fitted to manipulability—but which situate us, which render us ultimately passive. And in so doing, they suggest reality is like the opposite of what our technologies suggest reality is like, and therefore they make manifest entirely different dimensions of reality.

To summarize, my argument has been that the common response to materialism, which involves defending certain Aristotelian positions and noting the historical circumstances in which Aristotle was prematurely dismissed, must (for the sake of persuasion, which is not to say correctness) be supplemented by an account of why it is that materialism is a "live option" for modern persons. Even if one is persuaded intellectually that materialism is not cogent, it "feels" like a possible construal of things. Why? My argument is that we have been shaped to perceive reality this way by the technological order that we tacitly imbibe every day, in its

61

psyche-shaping act of reducing the real, *in all our practical involvements with it*, to the manipulable, observable, "visible" order. The most important point is that the world within which this is plausible is a world *shared* by both metaphysicians and materialists. And recognizing the shared structures of our involvement with the world, and the philosophical pressures implicit in that involvement, it is worth asking how bringing them to explicit recognition might help to change the debate between materialists and metaphysicians.

In my judgment, the implications of this argument, for materialism, are deflationary. By helping to explain what remains compelling about the materialist position even to those who don't hold to it, we have also tried to relativize its appeal against the background noise that both makes it attractive and simultaneously renders relevant philosophical analysis powerless in its persuasive charm. It is non-compelling because it is coded as belonging to a different order than the order of what is "real," the world in which I am immediately and practically and socially engaged. Once that construal of the real is relativized, so are its philosophically dismissive instincts.

But we are where we are. And even if our mind is persuaded of this, our instincts might not be. What are we do to? It is this question I hope to take up in my next chapter.

IV:

SEEKING, FINDING, AND BEING FOUND

THE PREVIOUS two chapters have been largely descriptive, and I hope this one will be, at least in part, prescriptive. Here I want to propose the Christian's calling in light of our struggles. Of course, this needs to be stated as a question as well. *Are* there distinctive emphases in Christian doctrine or practice which uniquely minister to persons who find themselves in this situation? Not surprisingly, questions close to the one we are addressed have their own market niche. Not a month goes by without a new tome on atheism, secularism, modernity, and the Christian's or religious person's calling and responsibility in light of these phenomena. Arguably, many or most of these contain implicit longings for a lost past or a hoped-for future. Many interpret our modern problem to be one brought about ultimately by causes as diverse as Augustine's Neo-Platonism, medieval nominalism, medieval worldliness, the humanism of the Renaissance, the mechanical philosophy of the Enlightenment, the individualism of the Reformation, or "the Russians!" etc. The world, we are sometimes told, used to be "sacramental," suffused with divine agency, but it is now flattened and textureless because we have inherited the disenchanted universe of early modernity. Without treating this matter at length, I would argue that this is all (at best) a half-truth. Certainly our assumptions about and comportment to the world have drastically altered the probability that we will tacitly sense agency and consequent "divinity" therein. But we should not romanticize the condition of our ancestors. The "enchanted" universe was not just enchanted but superstitious and devastatingly so. We cannot underestimate the extent to which an average Medieval person might have spent his life in the fear of non-existent entities and (not to be overly polemical) a church which threatened to wield a spiritual power that Protestants would later claim for God and His word and His gospel alone. However much we might want to recover a sense of the world as "suffused with God's presence and agency," this would largely be a sort of *second naivete*, a movement from juvenile skepticism to mature adulthood rather than from juvenile skepticism to childish fantasy. And indeed, I will herein insist that this middle stage of juvenile skepticism is necessary and important.

I myself have perhaps argued for a version of the above narrative—albeit emphasizing tacit background noises over overt ideas. I have argued, I suspect without much originality, that our modern plausibility structures have more to do with the technological world than with anything else. And yet, this is not, as such, a "fall narrative," wherein the hope is to recover some pre-technological world, as though our spiritual future depended upon our Ludditist aspirations. While much of the modern situation is unique and problematic, much of it is also good. There is no question about the relationship between modern technological advances and many fulfilled opportunities for reaching people with the gospel. More immediately, advances in medicine, in agriculture, in education have drastically improved the condition and quality of life of the average person living on earth. We in the West experience this, of course, still more than most of our international neighbors, and perhaps precisely to this extent, the problems and challenges I've been seeking to describe are largely ours. But suffice it to say that I want to suggest our goal should not be to "go back" to when we did not have all this. That is not going to happen. We are where we are, and, in the future, the technological apparatus will only become more prominent. That's the situation in which we find ourselves. It is both exciting and dangerous and will only get moreso on both counts. The question then becomes what a Christian response to this might be.

BASIC ORIENTATION

As an initial foray into this problem, let us consider the following proverb:

> Two things I asked of You,
>   Do not refuse me before I die:
> Keep deception and lies far from me,
>   Give me neither poverty nor riches;
>   Feed me with the food that is my portion,
> That I not be full and deny You
>   and say, "Who is the LORD?"
> Or that I not be in want and steal,
>   And profane the name of my God.[1]

---

[1] Proverbs 30:7-9, NASB.

Is it possible that a statement several thousand years old has something to say to late modern persons? Perhaps here we can put together both the ancient and the modern sense of "divine absence," seeing them as two modes of the same problem in different contexts. To wit, for those whose deepest experience is their own dependence, their own fragility, their own inability to take care of themselves, the tendency is to forget God's providence, promises, and provision—to steal and, rather than trusting God's goodness and generosity, to profane His name. For those who experience their own independence, abundance, no fear concerning whether they will get their next meal (etc.), the tendency is simply to "forget" God's being. Certainly, I don't think the author is talking about atheism (unimaginable as this would normally have been in the ancient world), but he is talking about a sort of "out of sight; out of mind" response to God. God is not the one with whom we have to do because our world of concern is "full." In the words of that wonderful speech in the film *Network* (Sidney Lumet, 1976), we have "all necessities provided, all anxieties tranquilized, and all boredom amused."

In our situation, our world of concern has become so suffused with the illusion that we control it that we do not just forget God the way we forget a friend; we risk forgetting why we ever thought He was our friend in the first place, the way an adult can't quite recall whether certain childhood memories are childhood memories, dreams, or projections. Whatever the case, the plausibility of God is often as ephemeral and fragile as a vapor.

That is, *unless we remember*. This is the movement of many Psalms. In the moment of crisis and in a context wherein what "seems real" is defined by the immediate, the Psalmist must pause, be still, and re-situate his own immediacy in the context of deeper truths which are both close to the Psalmist objectively and far away from him psychologically. And so the Psalmist struggles. The Psalmist wrestles with God and, like Jacob, refuses to stop until God blesses him (Gen. 32:26). That is what modern Christians must do. We must wrestle with the angel until we emerge from the struggle with a new surety.

And I want to argue that the following is absolutely key. This kind of remembering is an act of will. We must address this at some length. The practice of remembrance is an act of the will. I have argued that we can be intellectually persuaded of God's being while still having a sense of His un-reality. Our tacit "sense of things" can be in tension with our intellectual grasp of them. And the context which sustains this tension is not going to change any time soon. It is what it is. What *can* change is *us*. Not in the sense that technologically mediated reality will not continue to find its echo in us, any more than the figure of an attractive member of the opposite sex will ever cease to be attractive to us. But take this latter example. If we have a strong tendency to lust, how does that change? Certainly not through getting rid of attractive people. God forbid! Rather, *we* change. Think of the parallel. We know objectively that lusting is bad, that it objectifies another person, that it is not dignified, that it is not ultimately fulfilling to the wonder and freedom of pure sexuality— and yet this objective knowledge does not mean that in the moment of temptation (in a culture telling us thousands and countless times per day that our deepest fulfillment is to be found in objectification) that our *affective* sense of things is not largely in tension with what we know. It surely often seems very much like lust is better, more beautiful, more good than what we know to be good. What changes is not the fact of our temptation, not the background noise, but the human subject. And we find ourselves thrown into a world which requires training, exercise, discipline, and faithfulness to continually bridge the gap between our objective good and our subjective sensibilities.

In the previous chapter, I emphasized God as the highest object of the human mind. In this chapter, I want to emphasize that God is the highest object of human desire, of human longing. God is beauty and love and plenitude. When we seek God with both of these aligned, our minds and our wills (which are interacting but separate), then we are seeking God with our whole persons. And is this not what Scripture means when it refers to seeking God? Hebrews speaks of those who believe that God *is* and that He is the rewarder of those who seek Him (Hebrews 11:6). God desires to be sought by mankind.

Let us then finally get back to this clever girl at agnostic camp whom we considered in chapter one. The question is this: "Could God be more obvious than He is? Could He erase all atheism? Could He overcome all intellectual doubt in an instance?" Yes. Yes. And absolutely yes. But He doesn't. Why? *Because God is only interested in His revelation being clear enough for the purposes He has in revealing Himself.* That is to say, God's revelation is about God's rather than man's goals. And it is not man, therefore, who determines how clear He must be. Man's purposes are often at odds with those of God. As it turns out, God is actually not that interested in people simply believing that He exists. Think of the parallel of Jesus in the Gospels. How often does Christ actually conceal His teaching and His identity precisely because He knows that people will simply abuse His teaching or seek to manipulate His identity for their own ends? Christ is most clear to those who pursue, who hunger, who thirst—and he satisfies them, as in the case of the woman at the well (John 4). This does not mean that His identity was, as such, unclear. It means that He was not interested in maximal clarity. His clarity was fitting to His own purposes in coming and revealing Himself and His Father. So it is with God in natural revelation. God is not interested in people merely "believing" in Him (i.e. recognizing the fact of His existence). If they do, great. If not, they are not necessarily any worse off than if they had. Why would He then "fix" what isn't, by His standards, broken? Was, after all, that medieval world (suffused with divine agency, the so-called "sacramental universe") a world of godliness, of love for God, of pursuit of His kingdom? *Certainly not!* Was ancient Israel full of faithful Hebrews because God's cloud was in their midst? *Certainly not!* Was the New Testament church fine and dandy because they had the immediacy of the Spirit's movement? A cursory reading of Paul's Corinthian correspondence would suggest otherwise. In each of these cases, God's presence was "more clear" in some relevant sense than it is to us. And yet human beings were no different then than they are now. "If they do not listen to Moses and the prophets," Christ says, "they will not be persuaded even if someone rises from the dead" (Luke 16:31). Take note. Jesus is not talking about believing in God's existence or power but about believing "on" God as a child. The problem is and always has been the human heart. Intellectual distortion has always been a function of this more primal seat of human fallenness. What this highlights, then, is that while the temptation to atheism is not necessary a vice, *overcoming* that temptation nevertheless requires the formation of virtue.

So much could be said to elucidate this point. I fear that my reflections on this must be sporadic, suggestive, and terribly incomplete. Nevertheless, I will mention at least three important ways that the will is involved in remembering God.

THREE SPHERES OF ACTIVITY

First, in the context of our intellectual temptation, it is likely more important for us than for many of our spiritual forefathers to "go over" our reasoning again and again. This need not be done from a posture of doubt, but our minds do not float free of our bodies and our contexts and our stories, and without the exercise of reminding ourselves why we believe the things that we do, we will tend to make ourselves vulnerable to all of the tacit and explicit assaults on our faith. Below, I will suggest a list of three items concerning which we must constantly be re-persuaded.

Second, I don't think we can underestimate the importance of the church in our battle. Christ established a community (founded upon His Word), at least in part, to help and encourage one another. Like any community, the church can sometimes feel alienating to the doubting Christian (especially when everyone seems to "get it" while you don't). But it can also be "alien" in that it un-jams your reality signals so to speak. Often, simple statements from simple believers are encouraging, and help reorient us in the context of a sort of navel-gazing *ennui*—reminding us that we are but small and fragile men. Many who have lost their faith have been those who first abandoned assembling together with other believers, or who had become a psychological island which was not vulnerable to visitors. We cannot despise brothers and sisters in Christ who live in the same world that we do and whose attunement to it often far exceeds our own distorted calibration.

Third, we must mention the spiritual disciplines. If we must exercise our minds, if we must meet together with a community of practitioners, we must also exercise our bodies and our hearts in such a way as to reorient our loves, to reorient our sense of what is real and most valuable.[2] This also applies to corporate Christian worship (which then creates some overlap with my second point). But while the mind can be persuaded that a thing is true, it is often the disciplines and postures of the body, *faking it till you make it,* that actually reorients our more tacit sensibility. And this takes devotion, practice, and again, will. Marriage counselors know all about this. If a husband and wife are struggling in their marriage, and struggling to see good in one another, even though they know good to objectively be there—one practice is actually "deciding" to utter thankful words for your spouse. If a man commits to actively thanking God every day for five good things about

---

[2] James K.A. Smith's "Cultural Liturgies" project is helpful in this regard. See his *Desiring the Kingdom* (Grand Rapids: Baker Academic, 2009), *Imagining the Kingdom* (Grand Rapids: Baker Academic, 2013), and *Awaiting the King* (Grand Rapids: Baker Academic, 2017).

his wife and a wife commits herself to thanking God every day for five good things about her husband, their hearts will almost inevitably be reoriented because they are re-narrating the world to themselves, sending different signals which access those very same tacit neuro-plastic portals that process reality in general. Only, the difference is that this takes actively shaping our cognitive inputs rather than mere passivity as it pertains to our contexts and our emotions. In a word, it takes strategy.

THREE ACTS OF REMEMBRANCE

Let us, then, strategize together. I have thus far highlighted three ways in which the will is involved in the remembering of God. But what is the content of that remembrance? In what remains of this chapter, I will highlight three truths that must be constantly recollected. And indeed, such remembrance can also motivate us to take up the very spiritual practices which reorient us to the truths themselves, making them "seem" more plausible. A certain "construal of the world" is implicit and carried along in the practices. We are then reciprocally motivated to faithful practice to the extent that our persuasion and our will grow stronger. I will attempt to highlight this further below. In any case, let us strategize around the remembrance of following three propositions:

> *First*, God is *actus purus* or pure act.
> *Second*, God is *pro me*, or for me, in Christ.
> *Third*, human beings, made in God's image, are guilty of sin before God.

72

This is all Latin for "God is pure being, bliss, plenitude, infinity, greatness, holiness, perfection, love, active and eternal beatitude in the Father, Son, and Spirit," for, "Jesus loves me, this I know," and for "Don't worry. You're both much better off and much worse off than you think you are," respectively. Here is our call to remember. It is not so different than what the Psalmist must remember, though it might have distinctive applications in our context. And so, let us look at these in turn.

One of the things that the vision of God communicated in the previous chapter leads to is a conception of God that is deeply mysterious and absolute. God is Absolute Personhood who sustains the entire cosmos in being, who donates life to it and which, before Him, is but a drop. The atheist love for looking at big cosmic images is actually helpful here—he is "not far from the kingdom of heaven," we might say. The human is "haunted" by the *big* and the *other*, and the universe is so fantastically large. Its nooks and crannies are unimaginable and unimaginably beautiful. We truly cannot comprehend its vastness. And yet, before God, it is as nothing. From one end to the other, and in all of its parts, the universe is an incredibly specific *this* which could have been *that*. And yet. These *are*! *This* is! All of the incomprehensible vastness of being, the relation of each particular to each particular, obtains because God in His wisdom wanted *this* world, *this* universe, *these* physical laws, *this* human race, *this* history. We must cultivate this sensibility in us and in our atheist neighbors. The oceans are but a drop in His palm. The king's heart is in His hand. He rides on the storm. He controls the seas. Life and death are in His hands. He is unimaginable, simultaneously the highest object of human reflection and the rock bottom infinite concrete against whom human reflection smashes into pieces. If this is true (hear me out), how could we not expect mystery? Note, what I claim here is *not*—and I will insist on this—the capitulation of an intellectual punt. It is rather to say that if I am confronted with something I do not understand (and there are many things I am confronted with that I do not understand) God is not negated any more than the mystery of quantum field theory (which I also don't understand) is negated. What is more, such lack of understanding is precisely *what I'd expect* of my finitude attempting to grasp the infinite when I cannot even grasp a lot of the finite. The only world in which this could be rendered a philosophically unpardonable sin is a world which is irreducibly manipulable to my control, over which the human mind is a greater order of being, and human control a greater order of agency, etc. But we are absolutely dependent upon the free upholding of God's creative Word. We are a vapor.

It seems to me that the moment we grasp this, the moment we truly understand that it is metaphysically necessary that there be a God before whom we are all less than nothing (Isa. 40:17), the shape of our questions changes. He no longer stands before us as one owing an account. We stand before *Him*. It is fascinating to note the hubris of the modern problem of evil in this respect. Why do I call it modern? Isn't the problem of evil ancient? Yes, but take note. The problem of evil is presented as something like this: If evil exists, God cannot exist, be good, and be sovereign simultaneously. So which one do we let go of? We say that He doesn't exist! Or a lot of Christians claim that God is not absolutely in control. In the ancient world this would have been insane. Of course God exists! Of course He's in control! But is He good? That's what the Psalmist struggles with. That's what most of the world struggles with. Even if it is metaphysically necessary that God is, we are still left with that more ancient version of the problem of divine absence—and that is the question of His felt goodness. I will attempt to address this question directly below.

Dwelling on this first act of remembrance for a moment longer, however, I want to highlight that we do not have an imagination shaped to grasp this. That God exists and is great and mysterious means that the statement, "His ways are above our ways," is perhaps the height of rationality rather than the easy punt of laziness. It means that to see God is to say "whoa," "wow," and to know our own finitude. But our culture sends us thousands of messages a day which trivialize the greatest Good, which cultivate in us a mind and a heart that cannot even imagine such *gravitas*! Our world is awash in triviality and religion which reduces God to the shape of my wishful thinking. Inasmuch as modern atheists preserve this deeper sense of "wow-ness" about anything, they are (ironically) the best of modern Western religion.

In any case, once this is clear, what does that leave us with? Reality is what and as it is. And sometimes it sucks. Sometimes it is hard. Much of it is disintegrated by evil. Is God perhaps laughing? Is He an uncaring demon? A Father to be hated? And now we're talking. That's the real question, the deepest question, the right question, the best question! Let it be said—the *brave* question.

If our first remembrance took us to Aquinas' proofs, it only took us as far as a Muslim, a traditional Jew, a

Hindu, a Buddhist might go. Indeed, as David Bentley Hart shows, much of what I have argued so far would be agreed upon by them and excite them.[3] And yet Paul's statement in 1 Corinthians 15:32 haunts me. If Christ has not been raised, then we have no hope and we are still in our sins. If Christ has not been raised, then we must eat, drink, and be merry—for tomorrow we die. If so, this first point is not enough. God as *actus purus* must also be God *pro me*. If the former took us to Aquinas, the latter takes us to Luther.

"God is for you." The reason I know God is good is because God has actually sought to resolve human evil in Himself. The reason I know God is good is because He has forgiven my sins. The reason I know God is good is because Christ has been raised from the dead, the Spirit has been sent, and He is remaking the world into His kingdom (ultimately by crowning and purifying this order of things in the new creation—which is just this creation perfected and purified). This does not mean that I know why this particular evil event happened or why God didn't stop this or that evil thing. I don't. I suspect He actually does stop evil all the time. Naturally, we wouldn't notice evils He has prevented. But He doesn't stop all evil and He does allow many events which I don't understand. Why? I don't know why. But I do know why *not*.[4] And it is not because He is unconcerned. In Christ, we see the smiling face of God to the sinner who lives in ethical tension with Him. In Christ (let it be said from the rooftops!), God has

---

[3] See his aforementioned *The Experience of God*.

[4] I am influenced in this way of putting the matter by Tim Keller's helpful discussion in *The Reason for God: Belief in an Age of Skepticism* (New York: Dutton, 2008), 22-34.

sought us. We have not ascended to heaven; He has descended to earth. Christ is the presence of God to answer all divine absence. "Where are you? Where are you? Where are you?" The answer to this is a cross, a resurrection, a Spirit, forgiven sins, renewed life, and real eternal hope. No person has an answer to the problem of evil. But only the Christian message has a definitive answer to what the problem is *not*. As Eric Alexander once ended a sermon, "Who could ever want to be anything other than a Christian?"

Note how beautifully these two remembrances work together and go back and forth to one another. God is pure beatitude and love, pure actuality and being. And we find ourselves in a contingent world He did not need for Himself. He made it in love. It is already pure gift, pure donation, pure contingency, and pure freedom. Again, this *must* be. And yet we find ourselves in a situation wherein all is not well. *But it is a world into which we have, then, no reason to imagine God cannot (or would not) speak, intrude, etc.* Creation itself is already His free act. Revealing Himself is not a different sort of act. A miracle is not a different sort of power than the power it took to create in the first place. Divine speech is not "more impressive" than upholding a contingent world, which has no being in itself, by the power of His Word. The very shape of the puzzle piece of reality and our experience of it fits its complement in the special revelation of the gospel, that God is for us, that He is the rewarder of those who seek Him, and that He has ultimately sought us in Christ, that He continues to do so through his Spirit and through His mouthpiece, the people of God. What I want to highlight here is just how much the shape of what we agree upon with the sages of the nations actually resonates with and quite seamlessly is fitted to what is specially revealed in the gospel. Christ is indeed the hoped for Desire of the nations.[5]

Implied in the symmetry of these two remembrances is that any skepticism concerning God's desire and capacity to be "for me" in Christ and in the gospel can be converted into an incoherent cynical posture toward creation in the first place—which is also a pure donation of God's freedom. A God constitutionally unconcerned with man cannot be the God whom we know to be necessary. And the God whom we know to be necessary is shaped like and is echoed in the One whom the Scriptures call the exact representation of His being (Hebrews 1:3), the person of Jesus Christ who freely comes to redeem the finite world He loves.

Implicit in all of this, however, is our third call to remembrance. Human beings, made in God's image, are guilty before God. To say that God is interested in being sought by whole persons is not to say that whole persons often seek Him. Indeed, it is precisely what we don't do. And this is because we are in ethical tension with God. We actively see Him as an object to be manipulated for our ends rather than the end in Himself. Our minds and hearts stir with an ancient echo, but we fill them and distract them with thing after thing. We are creatures of distraction, and of a pathological sort. Our failure to seek God is not a warranted inference from the world as it reveals itself to us; it is, rather a sort of insanity of our

---

[5] For more considered reflection upon this theme, see my "Classical Theism in a World Come of Age," in *God of Our Fathers: Classical Theism for the Contemporary Church*, ed. Bradford Littlejohn (Moscow, ID: The Davenant Press, 2018), 207-32.

species—a refusal to eat and drink the real bread and wine for which we were made and which are ever before us and available, but instead to fatten ourselves on their artificial surrogates. It is really fun to read some of the sages of the world on this. They often detect these human problems, and diagnose them fairly well. But they propose all sorts of solutions in asceticism, discipline, new perspectives, harmony, balance, love, sacrifice, etc.—perhaps even claiming divine revelation along the way. But what remains suppressed among many of the sages is *guilt*. Let's face it. We cannot just "promise to do better." We have violated. We have sinned. We have failed. We stand before the Ground of our being as violators of God's bond with us, as contributors to the world's chaos. We are born in sin. Our race perpetuates ruination. And we cannot rightly grasp what a massive treason this is until we get God right. Sin is not trivial because God is not trivial. To reject the Fountain of all beauty and goodness, to whore ourselves after fake copies of the One in whom is our every breath, who is closer to our being than we are to ourselves, is cosmic treason (as R.C. Sproul once put it). It is absolutely *urgent* that we cultivate the psychological and intellectual capacity to feel this in our bones. It's not trivial. It's a problem. There is a violation that must be dealt with. There is *guilt*.

As we remember that God upholds us in being as a pure gift, we also recognize our own ethical tension with Him. And most of the world's sages fail to see this sufficiently as a problem. If, in our second point, Christ's work is the only moment wherein we see a definitive answer to what the problem of evil is not, it is also the only moment that actually captures sufficiently how bad evil itself is. The cross says that sin cannot just be ignored or made up for. We are guilty. And as Anselm famously argued, if you want to see how bad it is, look at the cost it took to fix. And now again, here we highlight the seamlessness of natural and special revelation—this time as it applies to our guilt. If God has made us freely and generously, and we are in ethical tension with Him, are we not dependent upon Him for our solution; not upon our ascent, but upon His descent, His further free act in defeating evil and in renewing us? The necessity of God Himself to intervene amidst human unfaithfulness has perhaps never been captured better than in the second chapter of Hosea's prophecy. Speaking to a constantly faithless, distracted, and idolatrous Israel, God speaks the following divine words:

> "Therefore, behold, I will allure her,
> Bring her into the wilderness
> And speak kindly to her.
> "Then I will give her her vineyards from there,
> And the valley of Achor as a door of hope.
> And she will sing there as in the days of her youth,
> As in the day when she came up from the land of Egypt.
> "It will come about in that day," declares the LORD,
> "That you will call Me Ishi
> And will no longer call Me Baali.
> "For I will remove the names of the Baals from her mouth,
> So that they will be mentioned by their names no more.
> "In that day I will also make a covenant for them
> With the beasts of the field,
> The birds of the sky
> And the creeping things of the ground.

And I will abolish the bow, the sword and war from
the land,
And will make them lie down in safety.
"I will betroth you to Me forever;
Yes, I will betroth you to Me in righteousness and in
justice,
In loving kindness and in compassion,
And I will betroth you to Me in faithfulness.
Then you will know the LORD.
"It will come about in that day that I will respond,"
declares the LORD.
"I will respond to the heavens, and they will
respond to the earth,
And the earth will respond to the grain, to the new
wine and to the oil,
And they will respond to Jezreel.
"I will sow her for Myself in the land.
I will also have compassion on her who had not
obtained compassion,
And I will say to those who were not My people,
'You are My people!'
And they will say, '*You are* my God!'"[6]

You can read all the other literatures of the world and
not read this. The God who broke through nothing and
made something intruded into this world to speak to our
forefathers, intruded into history to reveal Himself to
Israel, has intruded most fully and finally in Christ, His
cross, and in His resurrection. In Christ, God declares, "I
have taken your guilt here. I will forgive you here. I will
bind myself to you here." Many gods have exercised
mercy. But *here* God forgives His *enemies* by sheer grace,
not by ignoring the enormity of their crime, but by

---

[6] Hosea 2:14-23, NASB.

drinking His own righteous judgment in the Person of Christ to the very last drop. For all the items of the Christian faith that we might struggle to believe, is it plausible that *this* was the invention of men? It is too scandalous, and it is the positive side of the statement that God *does indeed* work in mysterious ways—praise God! Here we do not abrogate our critical judgment, but we adore His—finding in Christ divine actions which minister to reality as it actually manifests historically, corporately, and individually.

So, three remembrances. We are not left without questions. We have rather confronted reality as manifested in God's general revelation in nature and his special revelation in Scripture—and we are left reoriented to re-examine our questions. We are left as creatures, guilty creatures, asking questions to a God who is necessarily beyond comprehension, and who is demonstrably and irrefutably good—and who, if He cares about our guilt at the cost of His Son, cares about our whole selves and His whole creation. How will He not, with Christ, as Paul writes, freely give us all things (Rom. 8:32)? The God who would bear the curse in the Person of His Son cannot be a God who is unconcerned about the economy, about the welfare of a nation, about the triumph of justice, or (closer to home) that you want your child to get into a certain school, that you want a particular job, that you are lonely, that you are sick, that you have a headache. He might answer "no" to some of these requests for His own good reasons, but He has shown that He is God "for us."

God is for me. How do I know? Jesus.

V:

CONCLUDING REFLECTIONS

I WANT TO conclude with a few final reflections.

I have said already that we are left with not a new set of answers to our questions, but a new posture from which we begin asking the questions in the first place. There are lots of mysterious questions—concerning the relationship of humankind to Adam, how it is fair that we carry corporate guilt, how God can be sovereign over the cosmos and history and yet we can be responsible for our actions, how to interpret the boundary between evil and tragedy as the judgment of sin and/or as mere tragedy, etc. Many of us still struggle with these questions. But they all sit atop these basic demonstrable "in front of your face" facts. God is great beyond our comprehension. We are fallen, fragile, and contingent creatures who see the smallest bit of reality. And God has demonstrated Himself to be good. We do not see how it all fits together, but why should we? That would be asking us, perhaps, to understand how every property of the universe relates to every other property of the universe. I cannot, and you cannot, even *imagine* such a calculus. But I'm insisting right now that this is not a cop-out. It is a rational conclusion. It is necessarily the shape of reality, and therefore it necessarily confronts the questioner concerning the pedestal upon which they question. And we question as creatures who have been given enough for our pilgrimage. If Christ is not enough, then neither will you believe if *insert anything here*. This is not because reality is not clear enough. It is because our hearts are angry, which itself speaks to a deeper pathology and a demonstrably distorted and insane vision of the Good.

We must cultivate confidence about this. Not a confidence born of self-flattery or some inflated sense of their intellectual superiority. Not many Christians are wise and strong, Paul says (1 Cor 1:26). No, Christians should speak with a confidence born of confronting reality at its hardest edges. It is not that we couldn't be wrong inasmuch as we are creatures, it is that nevertheless we find ourselves confronted with reality in its clarity, and we can only echo it back. This is where the apologetics of the ordinary believer is so valuable. Most of them don't read a bunch of books. But they might be found saying things like, "Can't God just do that because He's God?" Many tomes could work out the mechanics of such a query, but they could not improve upon this fundamental and most basic insight. Many of our grandmothers are confident that God is because they are comforted when they are sad, joyful in their uncertainty, know a beauty amidst distortion, and a certain and unshakable truth (reality Himself) which cannot be obscured by men. Though this is perhaps to overly subjectivize the matter. The reason they are confident is not just because of God's comforting acts (though their comfort arises in part from that), but because of the relation of those acts to all of God's acts. The God in whom they trust is a God who is pure actuality, who

84

creates, speaks, organizes, directs, plans, intrudes, sustains, forgives, and has done so for all time and is available to them right there and then. In the Scriptures, trust in God is never abstract but is always connected to a pedigree of clear activities that reveal to historical and contingent creatures just who it is that they trust. Granny might not be competent to ward off objections to all of this, but inasmuch as the objections ultimately have basic reality and its historical manifestation in their sights, they are founded on nothing.

This orientation to and confidence in basic realities is particularly important when we confront the hard questions of Scripture and of theology. They're difficult. The Bible has lots of bits which are hard to understand and which might be thrown in our face as things which render us gullible. And what, of course, of other religions? What about the relationship of human responsibility to divine sovereignty? I have tried to present here a two-edged sword of a response to this. On the one hand, a reorientation to God Himself enables us to reassess what is ultimately plausible and implausible. And secondly, the shape of reality and its basic questions are spoken to in Christian revelation in such a way that Christ is shown to be the true and concrete myth, the center point of history, the Desire of the nations. In Christianity's emphasis on "God for me," and particularly "for me" in my and *our* most basic existential crisis (our singular and corporate guilt)—it echoes with the same voice of the one who called creation into being out of nothing.

This does not de-incentivize the pursuit of these questions, of course—anymore than the "basic truths" of a scientific paradigm de-incentivize trying to figure out the unclear bits. There are actually very helpful treatments of the difficult bits of the Old Testament, of the historicity of its events, of the relationship of God's sovereignty to human freedom, of the nature of corporate guilt, etc.[1] I cannot address these here, but I can suggest a prudential rubric for determining how to go about seeking answers to these questions: In my judgment, the best treatments of these questions show how these items are parallel to questions and problems which obtain whether or not Christianity is true. Why do human beings sacrifice? How do we understand human responsibility and freedom in any vision of the universe? Why are humans sometimes sympathetic to ideologies that portray the whole human race as a cancer which is destroying the earth? Is that a secularized corporate guilt? Are there modern versions of sacrifice? Find those treatments which ask and answer the questions on that level because *they* are simply dealing with reality. What is more, know the Bible and know it well. Most of the time, those who are trivializing or trying to embarrass you with the Bible are shallow readers and demonstrably so.

We can't look at all questions here. However, let us consider, one last time, the one which opened this volume. Let us once again ask, as dependent creatures (like Augustine in his *Confessions*) "Why it is that God doesn't

---

[1] See, respectively, on these issues, Joshua Ryan Butler, *The Skeleton's in God's Closet* (Nashville: Thomas Nelson, 2014); Iain Provan, V. Philips Long, and Tremper Longman, *A Biblical History of Israel* (Louisville: Westminster John Knox Press, 2003); Kevin Vanhoozer, *Remythologizing Theology: Divine Action, Passion, and Authorship* (Cambridge: Cambridge University Press, 2010), 295-386; Herman Bavinck, *Reformed Dogmatics Volume 3: Sin and Salvation in Christ*, ed. John Bolt and trans. John Vriend (Grand Rapids: Baker Academic, 2006), 75-125.

show up? Why does He allow me to struggle? Why won't He just appear when I need Him to, when I beg Him to?" I have said that God's clarity is suited to His purposes in revealing Himself. But why is He not interested in being more clear to me, who wants to know Him? Is His absence a divine judgment on this world? Certainly, that is a part of the answer, but even in the Genesis account, note that this is not entirely the case. In Genesis, God apparently "comes" and "goes" out of the garden even before the Fall. There is still some distinction between God's divine heavenly realm and man's earthly dwelling place. And while God descends into the garden as He later descended into Israel's tabernacle, God's presence is accompanied by God's absence. This is why God can say, "Where are you, Adam?" And Adam can say, "I heard you coming and I was afraid." In Israel, God comes and He goes. He is silent and then He speaks. He speaks to Abraham, Isaac, and Jacob, and then He is apparently silent as His people live in slavery for centuries. He shows up and redeems them, sets up a tabernacle, a priesthood, a kingship—then the nation of Israel goes into exile for this rebellion. Not long after the exile, God is apparently absent for several centuries again. And then He comes climactically in the Person of Christ. And yet even Jesus Himself, after the resurrection, ascends into heaven. Just when it would seem that God is finally with us permanently, He goes away![2] He bridges this absence through the Spirit, who feeds us as God fed His people manna in the wilderness. But even this is often

[2] Michael Horton reflects extensively on this in his *People and Place: A Covenant Ecclesiology* (Louisville: Westminster John Knox Press, 2008), 1-34.

experienced as an absence, a silence, a context that necessitates a trust which the Spirit works in us through Word, sacrament, and prayer. We long for that time which Scripture speaks of in Revelation 21-22, when heaven and earth come together, and the presence of God with man is permanent, when there is no absence (though perhaps never a lack of development or increasing presence—an ever aching for "more" of the infinite God in Christ).

But what is going on here? Why all this absence? Even in creation? Even in Christ?

I believe the answer to this is right in front of our face. We are contingent creatures who develop. We mature. And we mature and change and are perfected by means of shifting circumstances and their challenges. God actually gave Adam a task, to cultivate and keep the garden, to be fruitful and multiply, to fill the earth, subdue it, and rule over it. Adam was to grow in this. Adam was meant become a man, to be perfected and to be crowned with glory. In his failure, we failed. But this maturing structure is still built into us. The British sociologist, Anthony Giddens, for instance, writes about the way in which infants develop through their parents' absence as well as their presence,

> Crucial to the intersection of trust with emergent social capabilities on the part of the infant ... is absence. Here, at the heart of the psychological development of trust, we rediscover the problematic of time-space distanciation. For a fundamental feature of the early formation of trust is trust in the caretaker's return. A feeling of the reliability, yet independent experience, of others— central to a sense of continuity of self-

> identity—is predicated upon the recognition that the absence of the mother does not represent a withdrawal of love. Trust thus brackets distance in time and space and so blocks off existential anxieties which, if they were allowed to concretise, might become a source of continuing emotional and behavioural anguish throughout life.[3]

Note here that without absence, the very experience of "presence" is different. It is actually absence which makes presence more than a mere given. It is rendered a personal love, reliability, an agency which will never abandon us or fail to return, etc. God desires His contingent creatures to know this. And so He does not just create beatitude, but history—a history which involves a dialectic of comings and goings, presences and absences, our failures and His successes, precisely so that we will develop and be cultivated into the sorts of people He has made us to be. This is built into the very structure of things. And when we fail to mature, what does He do but enter into our humanity through Christ to bring it, in Him, to its intended perfection and glory? In Christ, the maturity which was always meant to be ours is achieved, our nature is perfected, and we are given the fruits of His labor through the Spirit who nevertheless then echoes this same narrative in us. Though Christ is the ultimate pattern, like Him, we suffer and grow and mature and enter the glory which He has already achieved. In some sense, locked herein are deep questions of why God has made history in the first place. Why is He interested in development, in

---

[3] Anthony Giddens, *The Consequences of Modernity* (Stanford: Stanford University Press, 1990), 97.

change, in something which goes from one stage to the next? To some extent this is built into the structure of finitude, but "history" is more than the mere capacity for change.

In any case, what does it mean when we find ourselves begging to see God and He does not show up? When He effectively and providentially says "no." It means, "My grace is sufficient for you. I've already shown up. I've already raised from the dead. I've already forgiven your sins. And just as I've done all this for your good, so for your good I want you to grow up. I want you to be strong. Trust me. I'll carry you. I will allow you to suffer. But I will carry you through. I will allow you to hit the bottom, but there you will find the eternal living and true God—and you will say with joy, 'This is enough.'" Like Job, you will be reoriented in the gravity of God. This is the reality that many of our grandmothers know, and it is a deeper insight than can be found in all of Aquinas. Indeed, Aquinas himself called all of his works "straw" compared to this simple personal knowledge of God—the Absolute Person.

And is this not, then, the counter-ethic to the attractiveness of the atheist "bravery narrative" in all its hubris? Can it be that we are brave enough to say that, in spite of evil, like the frightened child in the crib, in spite of raped children, in spite of racial tension, genocide, war, etc., that God is here and that He is good? Not as wishful thinking, not as calling evil "good," but as receiving reality just as it is and as it must be—despite what the world often feels like? Perhaps, indeed, atheism is not bravery after all, but capitulation. Perhaps it is an intellectual, spiritual, and psychological failure to *endure*. It is a failure to say that God, that the Good, is greater and denser and more fundamental and deeper and wider, that love is higher, that all is grounded in the infinite plentitude of a pure actuality which is love Himself—who is God "for us" through the trauma of rape to the discomfort of wrist pain. This is orientation to reality despite the mixed signals of our contingent order. This is precisely the sense I get when I meet those who confess God's goodness in the face of a death of a child, for instance. Each of us has met several people who do so from an unthinkable grief. And let's be honest, they often do not come off as though they "need a crutch," but as though they are deeply conscious that their story is not ultimate. Rather, God is ultimate and His goodness and eternal being are still greater realities and contain a greater gravity than death and pain.

Indeed, the Christian faith stands in profound critique of human avoidance. Humans avoid pain and suffering and doubt and insecurity. They avoid the truth about their world and about themselves. Even when they are honest, they stop short of the deepest diagnosis and hide the unsavory bits of reality. Christianity is profoundly human in its confrontation of the human and the human's world in its brokenness, fragility, and discomfort. These are not overcome through removal from finitude, from avoiding attachments—which is just to say an avoidance of love. We do love. We are attached. We stay in bodies. But our reality is not *the* reality. Our story is not *the* story. Our darkest selves are not avoided or smoothed over but recognized and then taken up into a greater Self and history. Which is not to say that we "see" it all through some pure act of intellection. We see only enough to have every reason to trust the fundamental goodness of being and of the Person who enacts His cosmic drama on its stage. Which is to say that we can trust chiefly because of a cross and a resurrection—without which all our musings and practices are vain.

A final thought concerning human practices. It has in fact *always* been true that the "reality," the "whoaness," of God is most clear to those who will God, to those who love and seek Him. This is not because He is more "obvious" in creation as such. Philosophy has always been able to establish the idiocy of our tendencies, our collective insanity (of which modern atheism is just a particular inflection). Rather, reality itself is more manifest to those who love because our "capacity to be revealed to" is enhanced. When one has a lover, they observe little things about him or her—not by inventing them, but by posturing themselves to have the sheer otherness of a person confront them in all its particulars. The best scientist is not the one who approaches with an agenda but whose study and observation are a crying out to be "revealed to," to "be confronted with." As you can see, our very way of stating what is happening in scientific observations makes all the difference for whether or not we consider creation "personal." Is it about us? Or are human beings that mysterious receptacle which is "spoken to" and which can refine our ears and our other faculties to listen for realities subtler voices? This is as true when we are trying to more deeply understand tree bark as when we are trying to more deeply understand God. Each attempt takes postures and practices and pursuits.

Failure to attend to the finer notes is not a function of their non-existence, but rather of our distraction, suppression, or of our treating them as insignificant. It is

92

virtuous to really want to learn and to know. And this hunger and virtue is formed through practices, communities, and through reflection. These *public* realities show our intuitions to be "odd" (in our case, atheism) but like ancient Israel in its own struggle with respect to divine absence, simply *knowing* that God is is not finally openness to reality. Rather, what is required is an openness and seeking which resonate with the frequencies at which *we are sought*. And this "being sought" shows up in both nature and in special revelation. The world manifests itself to us and will manifest more if we answer back with opening ourselves to it more—the way a good scientist refines the instruments of observation to increase their capacity to be revealed to. The instruments don't make the world, but only enhance our capacity to receive it. Similarly, God has spoken more clearly and ultimately in Scripture. And we know it and understand it the more we open ourselves to it as receivers. Here, God has spoken in Christ and we respond and are further able to listen, learn, and know more deeply. This ultimately takes the love of knowing and understanding. And we are, perhaps, as a culture, the worst listeners in history. We know, but we know shallowly. We are addicted to the quick and pithy. Just note most popular books on the Bible.

And indeed, when we listen to creation and we listen to God's speech in Scripture, it is discovered that we are not ultimately the seeker, but that we are being sought, that we can answer back, that He has stirred an unrest in us which opens up all of reality in its plenitude and beauty, and which, despite tragedy, is most fundamentally good.

Our seeking God is "middle-voiced," a doing which is more fundamentally a "done to." This gets us back to the "will" with which we started. God's pursuit of us is not akin to working on a machine, but He rather employs our agency, our creaturehood, our freedom. And it is precisely to His glory that, out of such freedom, He infallibly accomplishes His purposes in history and in eternity. Herman Bavinck says it masterfully this way:

> A freedom that cannot be obtained and enjoyed aside from the danger of licentiousness and caprice is still always to be preferred over a tyranny that suppressed liberty. In the creation of humanity, God himself chose the way of freedom, which carried with it the danger and actually the fact of sin as well, in preference to forced subjection. Even now, in ruling the world and governing the church, God still follows this royal road of liberty. It is precisely his honor that through freedom he nevertheless reaches his goal, creating order out of disorder, light from darkness, a cosmos out of chaos.[4]

---

[4] Herman Bavinck, *Reformed Dogmatics Volume 1: Prolegomena*, ed. John Bolt and trans. John Vriend (Grand Rapids: Baker Academic, 2003), 479.

BIBLIOGRAPHY

Bavinck, Herman. *Reformed Dogmatics Volume 1: Prolegomena*, Edited by John Bolt. Translated by John Vriend. Grand Rapids, MI: Baker Academic, 2003.

_____. *Reformed Dogmatics Volume 3: Sin and Salvation in Christ*, Edited by John Bolt. Translated by John Vriend. Grand Rapids, MI: Baker Academic, 2006.

Briggs, Carolyn S. *The Dark World: A Memoir of Salvation Found and Lost*. New York, NY: Bloomsbury, 2002.

Buckley, Michael. *At the Origins of Modern Atheism*. New Haven, CT: Yale University Press, 1987.

Burtt, E.A. *The Metaphysical Foundations of Modern Science*. Mineola, NY: Dover, 1932.

Butler, Joseph Ryan. *The Skeleton's in God's Closet*. Nashville, TN: Thomas Nelson, 2014.

Carr, Nicholas. *The Shallows: What the Internet is Doing to Our Brains*. New York, NY: Norton, 2011.

Cartwright, Nancy. *The Dappled World: A Study of the Boundaries of Science*. New York, NY: Cambridge University Press, 1999.

Channell, David. *A History of Technoscience: Erasing the Boundaries Between Science and Technology*. New York, NY: Routledge, 2017.

Clarke, W. Norris. *The One and the Many: A Contemporary Thomistic Metaphysics*. Notre Dame, IN: University of Notre Dame Press, 2001.

Dembski, William. *The Design Inference: Eliminating Chance Through Small Probabilities*. New York, NY: Cambridge University Press, 1998.

Dennett, Daniel. *Darwin's Dangerous Idea*. New York, NY: Simon & Schuster, 1996.

Ellul, Jacques. *The Technological Society*. New York, NY: Vintage, 1967.

Emonet, Peirre-Marie. *The Dearest Freshness Deep Down Things: An Introduction to the Philosophy of Being*. New York, NY: Herder & Herder, 1999.

Feser, Edward. *The Philosophy of Mind*. Oxford, UK: OneWorld, 2006.

_____. *The Last Superstition*. South Bend, IN: St. Augustine Press, 2010.

Feyerabend, Paul. *Against Method*. New York, NY: Verso, 2010.

Gaukroger, Stephen. *The Emergence of a Scientific Culture: Science and the Shaping of Modernity 1210-1685*. New York, NY: Oxford University Press, 2006.

Gay, Peter. *The Enlightenment: The Rise of Modern Paganism*. New York, NY: Norton, 1966.

_____. *The Enlightenment: The Science of Freedom*. New York, NY: Norton, 1969.

Giddens, Anthony. *The Consequences of Modernity*. Stanford, CA: Stanford University Press, 1990.

Gilson, Etienne. *From Aristotle to Darwin and Back Again: A Journey in Final Causality, Species, and Evolution*. Notre Dame, IN: Ignatius Press, 2009.

Hart, David Bentley. *The Beauty of the Infinite: The Aesthetics of Christian Truth*. Grand Rapids, MI: Eerdmans, 2003.

_____. *The Experience of God: Being, Consciousness, Bliss*. New Haven, CT: Yale University Press, 2013.

Heidegger, Martin. "The Question Concerning Technology." In *Basic Writings*, Edited by David Krell. New York, NY: Harper, 2008.

Horton, Michael. *People and Place: A Covenant Ecclesiology.* Louisville, KY: Westminster John Knox Press, 2008.

Keller, Tim. *The Reason for God: Belief in an Age of Skepticism.* New York, NY: Dutton, 2008.

_____. *Making Sense of God: An Invitation to the Skeptical.* New York, NY: Viking, 2016.

Kurzweil, Ray. *The Age of Spiritual Machines: When Computers Exceed Human Intelligence.* New York, NY: Penguin Books, 2000.

Larsen, Timothy. *Crisis of Doubt: Honest Faith in Nineteenth-Century England.* New York, NY: Oxford University Press, 2009.

Lelas, Srdjan. "Science as Technology," *The British Journal for the Philosophy of Science* 44.3 (1993): 423-42.

Lewis, C.S. *The Discarded Image.* New York, NY: Cambridge University Press, 2012.

Lindberg, David. *The Beginnings of Western Science.* Chicago, IL: University of Chicago Press, 2008.

Livingstone, David N. *Darwin's Forgotten Defenders: The Encounter Between Evangelical Theology and Evolutionary Thought.* Vancouver, B.C.: Regent College Publishing, 1984.

Minich, Joseph. "Classical Theism in a World Come of Age." In *God of Our Fathers: Classical Theism for the Contemporary Church*, Edited by Bradford Littlejohn. Moscow, ID: The Davenant Press, 2018.

Mumford, Lewis. "Science as Technology," *American Philosophical Society* 105.5 (1961): 506-11.

_____. *Technics and Civilization.* Chicago, IL: The University of Chicago Press, 1963.

Postman, Neil. *Technopoly: The Surrender of Culture to Technology*. New York, NY: Vintage, 1993.

Provan, Iain, V. Philips Long, and Tremper Longman. *A Biblical History of Israel*. Louisville, KY: Westminster John Knox Press, 2003.

Puckett, Joe. *The Apologetics of Joy: A Case for the Existence of God from C.S. Lewis's Argument from Desire*. Eugene, OR: Wipf & Stock, 2012.

Shanks, Niall. *God, The Devil, and Darwin: A Critique of Intelligent Design Theory*. New York, NY: Oxford University Press, 2004.

Shapin, Steven. *The Scientific Revolution*. Chicago, IL: The University of Chicago Press, 1998.

Smith, James K.A. *Desiring the Kingdom: Worship, Worldview, and Cultural Formation*. Grand Rapids, MI: Baker Academic, 2009.

_____. *Imagining the Kingdom: How Worship Works*. Grand Rapids, MI: Baker Academic, 2013.

_____. *Awaiting the King: Reforming Public Theology*. Grand Rapids, MI: Baker Academic, 2017.

Spitzer, Robert. *New Proofs for the Existence of God: Contributions from Contemporary Physics and Philosophy*. Grand Rapids, MI: Eerdmans, 2010.

Steiner, George. *Real Presences*. Chicago, IL: The University of Chicago Press, 1986.

Stenger, Victor. *God and the Folly of Faith*. Amherst, NY: Prometheus Press, 2012.

Taylor, Charles. *A Secular Age*. Cambridge, NY: Belknap Press, 2007.

Turner, James. *Without God, Without Creed: The Origins of Unbelief in America*. Baltimore, MD: Johns Hopkins University Press, 1986.

Updike, John. *In the Beauty of the Lilies*. New York, NY: Fawcett Columbine, 1996.

Vanhoozer, Kevin. *Remythologizing Theology: Divine Action, Passion, and Authorship.* Cambridge, UK: Cambridge University Press, 2010.

Watson, Peter. *The Age of Atheists: How We Have Sought to Live Since the Death of God.* New York, NY: Simon & Schuster, 2014.

Zuckerman, Phil. "Atheism, Secularity, and Well-being: How the Findings of Social Science Counter Negative Stereotypes and Assumptions," *Sociology Compass* 3.6 (2009): 949-71.

ABOUT THE DAVENANT INSTITUTE

The Davenant Institute supports the renewal of Christian wisdom for the contemporary church. It seeks to sponsor historical scholarship at the intersection of the church and academy, build networks of friendship and collaboration within the Reformed and evangelical world, and equip the saints with time-tested resources for faithful public witness.

We are a nonprofit organization supported by your tax-deductible gifts. Learn more about us, and donate, at www.davenantinstitute.org.

Made in the USA
Columbia, SC
19 June 2018